THE SANDWICH GENERATION

ADULT CHILDREN CARING FOR AGING PARENTS

CHARLES R. ROOTS

GARLAND PUBLISHING, INC.
A MEMBER OF THE TAYLOR & FRANCIS GROUP
NEW YORK & LONDON / 1998

Library of Congress Cataloging-in-Publication Data

Roots, Charles R., 1948–
    The sandwich generation : adult children caring for aging
parents / Charles R. Roots.
            p.   cm. — (Garland studies on the elderly in America)
    Includes bibliographical references and index.
    ISBN 0-8153-3004-9 (alk. paper)
    1. Middle aged persons—United States—Family relation-
ships. 2. Adult children—United States—Family relationships.
3. Aging parents—United States—Family relationships. 4. Aging
parents—Care—United States. I. Title. II. Series.
HQ1059.5.U5R66 1997
306.874—dc21   97-40761

Printed on acid-free, 250-year-life paper
Manufactured in the United States of America

Contents

PREFACE   ix

ACKNOWLEDGMENTS   xi

INTRODUCTION   3

THE SANDWICH GENERATION: A
CONTEMPORARY PROBLEM   5
    A Brief History of Parent Care   7
    Family Life Cycle   10
    Financial Woes   13
    Medical Insurance   17
    Physical Fitness   18

WILLING AND ABLE: WHO'S RESPONSIBLE FOR
    WHOM?   25
    Ethnic and Minority Cultures   25
    Legislative Pressure   26
    The Caregiver: Always on Call   27
    Sandwiched Sensitivity: A Sense of Humor Helps   36

HONOR THY FATHER AND THY MOTHER: AN
    ETHICAL PARADOX   43
    Honor and Dishonor: The Issue of Abuse   44
    Elder Abuse   46
    The Dysfunctional Family: A Crisis in Family
    Cohesiveness   49
    Feelings of Guilt: A Shared Complaint   51

MULTIPLE GENERATIONS: MULTIPLE
   SANDWICHING   53
   Medical Milestones   55
   Alzheimer's Disease: Who is this Person?   56
   The Right to Die (Euthanasia)   64
   Single Parent Families   66
   The Bottom Line: The Family Matters   68

THE ROLE OF THE CHURCH: A VIABLE MINISTRY?   73
   The Church Must Fill the Gap   73
   Teach the Church to Honor the Elderly   74
   Concerns of the Aging   78
   One Church's Example: Value Statements   80

EDUCATION OF THE SANDWICH GENERATION:
A BLUEPRINT   83
   A Twelve-Week Course   84
   LifeStories: All in the Family   87
   Just In Case   88
   Does Caring Ever Stop?   89

CONCLUSION AND ANALYSIS   93

SUMMARY   97

APPENDICES   101
   A. Helping Agencies   101
   B. Sandwich Generation Questionnaire   103
   C. Some Suggestions for Caregivers   105
   D. Elder Care: When the Folks Need Care and You're Not
      There   107
   E. Geriatric Glossary   111
   F. Twenty Drugs the Elderly Should Not Be Using   115
   G. Death Rates for Ten Leading Causes of Death Among
      Older People, By Age: 1988   117
   H. Estimated Long-Term Care Spending for All Age
      Groups, By Source: 1993   119
   I. Additional Resources   121

BIBLIOGRAPHY   127

INDEX   135

Preface

Personal experience is an excellent teacher. My first encounter as a member of the sandwich generation revealed that I had a great deal to learn.

I grew up holding very strong convictions about the role of the family and the responsibilities of the individual members. Quite simply, you take care of your own.

These convictions are ones I still hold strongly to, yet they have been tempered by some of life's harder experiences. In the early 1980's I was pastoring my first church in Fresno, California, when my step-father experienced heart trouble and required hospitalization and the insertion of a pacemaker. My mother was his primary caregiver, requiring my wife and me to become the primary caregivers to my ninety-three year old grandmother who had been living with my parents from the time I was ten years old. In other words, my mother had her mother-in-law living in her home for twenty-three years. Now I had my grandmother, who had in the previous two years experienced the full onset of Alzheimer's Disease.

It would be an understatement to say we had difficulty adjusting. My wife, Isaura, and I had two small children at the time, ages six months and three-and-a-half. My day was primarily taken up with ministry and the needs of the congregation. Isaura, on the other hand, literally had her hands full! After several stressful months with my grandmother in our home, it became quite clear that something had to be done. She needed to be watched twenty-four hours a day. She didn't know who any of us were any longer, and I had been her favorite grandson. She constantly demanded to be taken to the train station so she could return to Boston, her home town. She wanted to see her friends (none of whom were still living), and her Aunt Georgie, a close relative of hers who died sometime in the 1930's.

My wife never complained about this unbearable situation, holding to the same family values that I did. But there was a cumulative effect upon her that troubled me. Her own health has always been fragile, so it is imperative that she be allowed to rest. This, however, did not fit into my grandmother's daily regimen and work ethic. If she saw my wife lying down for a nap, my grandmother would walk over to shake her awake and declare, "You're too young to be taking naps. Get up!"

Please understand, this was not the way my grandmother was before Alzheimer's did its work. She was a very loving and gracious lady and would be horrified to know she had been so inconsiderate to my wife. Something had to be done . . . soon!

This was our initiation into the sandwich generation. We were one generation taking care of two generations: our children and my grandmother.

My stepfather and mother realized it would not be possible for my grandmother to come back to their home, and she couldn't continue with us. We finally did, what was to my way of thinking, the unthinkable. We actually gave serious consideration to having her put in "one of those places." I was heartsick. All my years growing up she had been my best friend. Now I was looking to place her in a nursing home.

We located a very nice facility that would provide her with the continuous supervision she required, and it was only a short distance from where we lived. When the day arrived for us to take her to the nursing home, I could hardly bring myself to look at her. She pleaded with us not to take her there. She wanted to stay with us, she said. My parents are the ones who wanted to admit her so my wife and I stayed home. I was so overcome with emotion that I retreated to our bedroom and stood there next to the bed and wept loudly for some time. My wife stood with me and held me close, knowing how much I hurt.

My grandmother was fine in her new location, adjusting to the new schedule without much difficulty. I, however, found it next to impossible to bring myself to make a visit to her. On the few occasions when I did visit, she would always ask me to take her out of "that place." The irony was that she didn't even remember I was her grandson. This is not the way I wanted to remember her.

Mercifully, she lived less than a year after being placed in the nursing home. Though I know in my mind we made the right decision in caring for my grandmother, my heart hurts to this day.

Acknowledgments

Thanks to my sandwich generation dialogue group for their candidness in sharing their numerous struggles, scattered joys, and countless tears while relating their efforts to survive the pressures of the sandwich generation. The dialogue group consisted of: Bob Boyd, Randy and Lori Hopkins, Cindy Lundell, Barbara Murphy, Janice Ormande, Dr. Gordon Rasmussen, my wife, Isaura Roots, Rocio Rubio-Busby, Rene and Sylvia Salazar, Roger Soderstrom, and Ginny Young.

Thanks to Anita Domries and Gary Frede for their invaluable assistance in tracking down and locating reference material.

Thanks to Rocio Rubio-Busby for her expertise in nursing care for the elderly, and providing me with excellent resource material.

Thanks to Elaine Walker for her marvelous patience and superior knowledge in being able to walk me through all the fine points in completing this book.

Finally, thanks to my mother, Christine Lake Garratt, for her steady, confident belief in me.

The Sandwich Generation

I
Introduction

I really don't want to live past 80. Eighty is old enough.
                                          Ethel "Bambi" Garratt, my grandmother

At the time my grandmother spoke these words I was a young teenager full of energy and anxious to see what was to become of my own life. She, on the other hand, was in her mid-seventies, living in her son's home, he being my stepfather. I wondered then, and I have often wondered since, why my grandmother would utter such a statement. I have observed a number of reasons why she might not be interested in living past fourscore years.

- She was widowed at age 61.
- She had trouble taking care of her large, three-storied house in Concord, Massachusetts.
- She came under her son's roof.
- She was convinced she should no longer drive. (She had a '40 Plymouth ragtop!)
- She had already outlived many of her contemporaries.
- She was experiencing minor illnesses.
- She had recently endured major surgery.
- She no longer lived in her hometown or cultural surroundings.
- Even while living with us she was still quite lonely.
- Due to my stepfather's business, we often moved from familiar areas.

Curiously, I find myself in a similar situation with my own mother who is now eighty-two years old. She is able to function quite well at a level that would exceed most her age. Yet certain illnesses have had varying affect, often halting physical activity or outside involvements. At times in the recent past she has struggled with a series of nagging illnesses, which, collectively, are quite debilitating. Having been a widow for five years now, she moved two years ago out of her home and into her own apartment just five minutes away from us. She is still a very competent driver, though this has caused me some concern at times. Her social life is centered around her children, grandchildren and church. She is actively involved in volunteer work, spending two or three days a month helping at the local hospital, and also tutoring a 40-year-old construction worker through the Adult Literacy Program.

The responsibility for literally taking care of my mother is not yet a reality. But in another way it is. Is she as prepared for unseen eventualities as she should be? Am I in a position to be of assistance to her, apart from moral support? How much (if any) of her life am I really responsible for anyway at this point? Does she want me to be more involved than I am? When do I parent my parent?

These questions and a host more are what invade my thinking, often uninvited and unwanted. Though I am addressing the subject of the right to die (euthanasia) in Chapter 5, it is presented only for the purposes of considering all aspects having a major effect on caring for elderly parents while taking care of children still at home. Most of us have a general idea of how to raise children in the home, but just how do you care for an elderly parent? The focus is on the family, and the responsibilities that are based on scripture, society, and family upbringing. The thrust of this book is to ferret out the real issues of being a parent to both your children and your parent(s). I find myself in what is more commonly being called the sandwich generation.

II

The Sandwich Generation:
A Contemporary Problem

Caught up with the challenges of raising a family and then starting a career, young adults often fail to notice that their own parents are growing older. When we reach middle age, these parents often begin to lose their health, their freedom, their financial stability, and at some time their mates. Parents, therefore, become more dependent, often at the time when their grandchildren are facing the struggles of adolescence. Middle-aged adults find themselves in what has been called the "sandwich generation," a time of life when we feel caught and sometimes torn between two generations, one older and one younger, both of whom have needs for help and guidance. This can create added pressure in middle age, along with the constant reminders that we all are growing older.[1]

The sandwich generation is a contemporary problem in that it has become the norm in an aging American society. Certainly in the past families took care of their elderly parents. But not so many folks lived as long then, and there were usually more family members to take care of fewer parents than there are today. Since there is a decrease in the numbers of offspring in recent generations, Social Security was developed as a mitigating factor.

It has been reported that at any given time in our country one out of three women live alone, whether by choice, or death of a spouse. "Recent figures (1978) show that the United States has more than eleven million widows and widowers, more than one million of them under fifty years of age."[2] Obviously, many of those who are widowed will remarry which is only a temporary solution in the care of elderly parents. What role and responsibility do the adult children have to their new stepparent? Once again, with the ever increasing age of the elderly, the responsibility for taking care of them will, undoubtedly, be placed on society as a whole.

Historically we can see that life expectancy, or the number of years an individual will still have to live, has altered greatly for society. In approximately 2000 B.C., the predicted average life expectancy was 18 years. By the year 1000 A.D., it was age 22. During the Middle Ages, it was thought to be 33 years, the eighteenth century 35.5 years, the nineteenth century 40.9, until today it is estimated to be approximately 75 years. By 1954 life expectancy was predicted to be 70 years, and, in the 1980's, it was reaching 73+ years (Census Bureau, 1983). In the 1980's, 29 million elderly comprise 12 percent of the population and one-sixth of all adults are 21+ years. Life expectancy of a newborn is approximately 75 years. The median age has increased to 31.2 years. The number of Americans 65+ surpassed that of the teenage population in 1983. Birth rates have dropped so low that Americans are no longer replacing themselves. Were it not for its immigrant population, the population of the United States would not be replacing itself. Americans are living longer. Twenty-eight million Americans were at least age 65 in 1984 representing 12 percent of the total population. Sixty percent were women (Perspective on Aging, 1986). The projected population for the 65+ age group is now estimated to be 32 million people by the year 2000, and over 35 million by year 2020 with an average of 51.4 years. . . .

Our society is getting increasingly older at an accelerated pace as these statistics would indicate. We not only find ourselves in a sandwich generation predicament, but there now exists the imminent potential for multi-sandwiched generations. . . .[3]

There are now more elderly than ever. They are living longer, and the oldest are living longer with increasingly severe disabilities and dependency needs. According to a 1983 U.S. Census Bureau Report, a person who was 80 at that time could expect to live another 8.2 years (1983). Four-generational families will soon be commonplace, which means that middle-aged 'children' could be faced with regularly helping their aging parents and their very elderly grandparents. By the year 2030, one out of every five U.S. Americans will be over 65: 10 percent of the population will be 75 years of age or older.[4]

As the previous quote clearly indicates, many more Americans are living longer, thus requiring care in varying degrees. The mantle of responsibility still rests with the family, and the traditional caregiver is still the woman. Whether this will change or not, or whether men will step forward in more of a caretaking role is impossible to say. As much as the state is presently involved in caring for the elderly it would seem to be logical that this trend would continue for a time. Americans are no longer replacing themselves, which raises concern for who is going to take care of the aging family member. Will it be the state, or the family?

Many baby boomers who have delayed childbearing are currently finding themselves faced with a double dilemma - caring for young children and aging parents at the same time.[5]

In his book, *Keep the Fire!*, Don Anderson writes to senior adults on approaching their senior years with perspective and passion.

> America is graying. . . . literally. The first wave of baby boomers has already crashed upon the shores of mid-life. Their parents, a generation beyond that milestone, are senior adults. With advances in health care and medicine, people are living longer. Senior adulthood, and consequently, retirement, can last a long, long time.[6]

A BRIEF HISTORY OF PARENT CARE

The care of elderly parents has historically been the responsibility of the adult children. In nonindustrial times, care for the aging family members was just one more part of a rural, agrarian culture. Once parents were no longer able to perform the chores around the home or work in the fields, they moved out of the main house and into a smaller home, usually located behind the main house. They remained an integral part of the family life. Even though they no longer held a position of productivity, they usually held the position of power, which meant they held the deed to the farm. If for no other reason than this, they were respected and honored.

Today many elderly persons no longer enjoy the respect of family and society. When they are no longer productive, they are virtually shunned by everyone, including Wall Street and the government. Even though they are significant in number, and enjoy a powerful lobbying base, there is not a wholesome regard for the elderly apart from their power monetarily and politically.

> It is rare to find an intact family surrounding the older adult. Children and other members of the family have often moved away from the nucleus of the family. Often they live out of town and/or out of state. If they still do live in the same town, they frequently have lost daily interaction with their older adults. This usually produces distance, misunderstanding, and, oftentimes, long-standing conflicts, which create strained relationships in the family. The older adult who is not the typically perceived ideal older adult is even further removed from the consideration of the family. Many civilizations revere their elders; America does not.[7]

Elder parents in bygone days were not expected to live as long as they do today. In the statistics quoted previously, the average age of adults in the nineteenth century was 40.9 years. However, there were many reasons why the life expectancy was so low. Only in modern times have we been able to eliminate many of the deadly diseases and pestilence that ravaged entire communities, skewing life expectancies. As a result of such medical milestones, in less than 100 years time the average age of life expectancy in the United States has nearly doubled (75 years). But until such advances were made in health care allowing the real possibility of extended life, young adult children did not really have to take care of aging parents because the parents died at a much younger age. These young adult children were raising their own young, while the elder parents were still working, oftentimes up to the day they died.[8] Working until the end of life had more to do with a social ethic and an established way of life, combined with the reality that no social organizations were available through the government as they are today. Churches and other helping agencies often fulfilled this responsibility. However, this means of caring for others gradually diminished.

Some family historians have postulated that conditions for family relations were not always so agreeable as we sometimes imagine. "Michael Gordon . . . reminds us that generational issues are not new; as late as the eighteenth century older people were considered a nuisance and a family liability."[9] Though the situation for today's family has been dramatically affected by the extended aging of parents, Jamia Jasper Jacobsen contends that the family is still the one key element in caring for the elderly.

The family still remains the cornerstone of caring for our elderly. While most aging parents do not live with their children, the responsibilities remain with the children to provide care, inspiration and help for them. "Though most may not share a household with their adult children, still 84 percent of people 65 or older live less than an hour away from one of their children, and four out of five see an adult child as often as once a week, two-thirds, as often as every day or two."[10]

Another factor in the historical change in family care is seen in the advent of industrialized America. Families now move to where jobs are available, most times in the urban areas of society. This means extended families are separated by distance and economics. For example, elderly, retired parents living on a fixed income, often cannot hope to live in the same neighborhood as their son or daughter who may very well enjoy a financial status that the parents never dreamed possible. The opposite may well be true also. Yet another factor is the surge of women into the work force in the last three to four decades. This has certainly helped the family's financial base, while at the same time leaving the home empty for extended periods of time each day. Ken Dychtwald says the situation for the sandwich generation does not look promising.

> Of all older Americans who need care today, 80 percent will receive that care from their families. Caring for a needy, aging relative has never been so difficult, prolonged, or common. As Lillian Troll of Rutgers University has written, "Adult children now provide more care and more difficult care over a much longer time than such children did in the 'good old days.'" A recent Boston magazine cover story that was devoted to parental caregiving had as its subhead: "You know you're really an adult when your parents need you more than you need them." Here, as elsewhere, aging is to a great degree a women's issue. Currently, of all adult-children caregivers, it is estimated that nearly 90 percent are women. The average age of these caregivers is 57, and more than one-third are 65 or older. The average American woman can

expect to spend more years caring for her parents than she did caring for her children.[11]

Historically, then, women have been the primary caregivers to elderly parents. Will this still be so in light of the changes taking place in society? All the evidence now shows that our society is shifting more and more to an adult orientation and away from a child orientation. "In the nineties the cultural center of gravity will migrate even farther into the realm of mid- and later-life concerns. Already, 10 percent of today's senior citizens have children who are also senior citizens."[12]

Parent care has only become a major issue in America within the last few decades. The experts all agree that this care is essential, and that it must be adequate. But who's going to provide this care? And who's going to pay for it?

FAMILY LIFE CYCLE

It is well understood that families will go through a life cycle, whether they are intact or fragmented, functional or dysfunctional.

> All families. . . . pass through certain predictable events or phases. . .
> but may also be confronted suddenly by unexpected events (financial
> reverses, teenage pregnancy, birth of a defective child). Such crises
> disrupt the family's normal flow of development and inevitably
> produce relationship changes within the family system.[13]

The concept of a family needs to have some definition and boundaries so that it is understood when the term "family" is mentioned. David Switzer, professor of pastoral care and counseling at the Perkins School of Theology, Dallas, Texas, describes the family as a system.

> Families aren't just groups of individuals. They are a group of people
> with ties to one another, who need to get many (and, for small children,
> almost all) of their important needs met within the family group.
> Therefore, they have a serious investment in maintaining the whole
> group so they can continue to meet one another's needs. The family is

an operational system. What affects one member affects not just other individuals *within* the system, but the whole *system* itself.[14] [italics in original]

Family therapist E. M. Duvall, has developed the family life cycle using a circle with eight sectors, each representing a time segment. In identifying these sectors, Duvall allows for a span of twenty-eight years from the time the first child is born to the departure from the home of the last child. "Note especially that about half of an average family's life is spent with children at home, half with husband and wife alone."[15] He allows for a fifteen-year period before retirement and then old age, which can cover another ten or more years.

Another view of the family life cycle has been developed by E. A. Carter and M. McGoldrick. In their view, "a family system encompasses at least three generations."[16] This ties in well with the sandwich generation dilemma since the difficulties associated with this generation are complex and unpredictable. Carter and McGoldrick further explain their position.

Although the typical American family maintains its own two-generational household, the members of that family are bound to react to past, present and future relationships within the three-generational family system. Life cycle transitions affect all members simultaneously as grandparents cope with the problems of old age, parents are dealing with the departure of their last child, "the empty nest," and the children are attempting to become independent adults. The events occurring at any one stage of the life cycle have a powerful influence on relationships at another stage.[17]

In an article on the Internet by Brooks Clark, this cogent statement clearly identifies the dilemma faced by today's sandwich generation.

If you've never been faced with caring for an elderly parent or relative, you may not have an up to date picture of senior care in the 90s. But statistics indicate there's a good likelihood that sooner or later you will. By 2000, nearly half of all working-age people in the country will have some day-to-day responsibility for elderly parents.[18]

The forces at work in the family structure can be opportunities to strengthen the bonds of the family, or a means of tearing it apart. Healthy families are those that can face the trials of life together by encouraging and supporting one another. Those that do not have a healthy family structure are practically doomed to failure since life is often most unfair as well as unpredictable. The pressures of life that are brought to bear will surely find the weak spots in the family structure.

In an effort to assist families who may one day find themselves facing the possibility of caring for aging parents I have intentionally focused on premarried couples and young marrieds since they are the next ones to find themselves in the sandwich generation. In fact, there exists the problem of multiple generations being cared for by one generation. This issue will be addressed in Chapter 5. If we can help these young couples early on in anticipating the problems they may encounter, not only in their marital relationship, but in the sandwiched potential they may face fifteen to twenty years down the road, we will have provided a valuable service. Even to get them thinking about such matters will have served a useful purpose.

Because couples may get off to a rough start in their marriage it is the intent of my ministry to assist these couples every way possible. In an effort to not only provide premarried couples with counseling I also have set up several other helpful programs. All of this is intended to be proactive in handling potential crises.

In the process of working with families, specifically premarrieds, the administering of personality and temperament analyses is given so as to have a picture of where the couple may encounter difficulties. I use the *Prepare/Enrich Inventories,* and the *Taylor-Johnson Temperament Analysis.*[19] It has proven to be most helpful in providing couples with a visual image of their lives as individuals compared to that of their mate. Particularly insightful is the *Prepare/Enrich Family of Origin Circumplex Model.* This reveals a person's family background and how they are likely to react to life situations.

Recently I was counseling a young couple planning to be married and was reviewing their *Family of Origin Circumplex Model.* I pointed out that the young man was located on the chart in the *Rigidly Disengaged* [italics mine] area. I discussed with this couple his family background and the ways his family handled conflict resolution. I asked him if the description of him being rigidly disengaged was accurate in the handling of conflicts. He acknowledged that it was very accurate. I then turned to his fiancee and asked her if she understood that this was his way of handling unpleasant situations. She indicated that she was aware of this. I advised her to keep this in mind for the future when conflicts would arise. Having recently performed their wedding I will be meeting with them in six months to do a marital checkup, which is one of my requirements. In particular, I will be asking them about their handling of conflict and its resolution.

In another counseling case I met with a couple planning to be married and went over with them their *Prepare/Enrich Inventory* and *Taylor-Johnson Temperament Analysis*. At the end of the session, it was clear to me that the woman was surprised by some of the man's responses in discussing the results of their assessment. A few days later she confided that she had broken off the engagement because the assessment had brought out some of the fears she sensed in the relationship, compounded by his responses.

FINANCIAL WOES

It is difficult to discuss parent care without immediately wondering how the bill is going to be paid. This is an area of great sensitivity and must be addressed if families can ever hope to be successful in caring for an elderly family member.

Caregiving children often give money as well as time. Because most long-term illness is not covered by Medicare or other government insurance programs, adult children often find themselves paying crippling medical expenses, or the expense of a stay in a convalescent home, which averages $20,000 to $40,000 per year. The problem is even greater for minorities. The proportion of older blacks, Hispanics, and Native Americans is growing at a much faster rate than that of older white Americans. The poverty rates of older minorities are far higher; in addition, their health is, on the average, worse, and they have less access to health care and helpful community programs.[20]

Reflecting on the historical mode of parent care, Pauline Regan makes several poignant statements concerning who has power and control.

> Before the advent of social security, children served as an insurance (the only insurance) against the hardships of old age. Parents counted on children to support them. Their trust in filial piety was well placed, because parents in their last years might still exercise control over their children's lives. In agricultural economics, one's livelihood and marital prospects depended on parents' willingness to turn over the family farm to sons or provide a dowry to daughters. Although a father might give his son permission to marry and settle on his land, the father maintained the property deed until his death. Even the last will and testament which transferred the ownership of land bound the heir to filial responsibility. Aging parents no longer have much economic clout over the behavior of their offspring. They rely on good will or guilt to motivate their children to live up to their expectations. For one thing, social security has liberated older people from abject dependence on younger family members. Regardless of the closeness of their family ties, the old can count on some minimal level of support. The old are no longer so vulnerable to the demands of the children, and the young need no longer fear the caprices of their elders. In short, economic changes have moved families along to a point where togetherness rests on tender sentiments, not grudging necessity. This also means kin who don't get along can afford to ignore one another.[21]

In one very touching story, Jim Ewing recounts how he and his father had been forced to make major decisions for the continued care and well-being of his parents. Both parents had been strong, independent people, yet age took a toll on them at the same time. It became apparent that both needed to be placed in a nursing home.

> We talked of the decision about the nursing home, the conversation with Mother, and alternate plans for his care. We planned the closing of the house for the winter and the management of the finances. We agreed that I would take over the financial record keeping, payment of the bills, and arrangements with the property and bonds. He was now placing in my hands an important part of his self-sufficiency, the management of his financial affairs.[22]

In her book, *Help! I'm Parenting My Parents*, Jamia Jacobsen includes an excellent chapter on finances entitled, "The Financial Perspective for the Aging Parent." Financial concerns affect everyone, but especially the elderly. Their years of high productivity are gone, and unless they have planned for retirement, they are locked into a fixed income bracket. Jacobsen's book is written as a "how-to" in looking after aging parents. It is much more practical than it is philosophical. Since she herself went through the struggles of parenting her parents, she was encouraged to write just such a book. To her dismay, she had found nothing written with "how-to" in mind. Thus, the chapter on finances is most helpful. The elderly "focus their energy on activities that reflect their health and wealth. They want to be assured that the wealth they have accumulated is wisely invested to allow them to retain their independence."[23]

According to Jacobsen, there are several "financial phases" to life. First, there is the "accumulation" phase. This phase is the time period when we use our resources to acquire assets or accomplish specific goals in life. Second, the "preservation" phase is the time when we have retired or no longer have a steady source of income. The attempt here is to maintain our lifestyle without expending all of our resources. "Most retired Americans are not so lucky, primarily because they were unable to effectively balance their savings/investment needs with spending pressures during the accumulation years."[24] Added to the problems in this phase is the ever-changing and increasing cost of living. The next phase is the "distribution" phase. Unpleasant as this is, with the shroud of mortality that hangs ominously over such a phase, the decision as to where our resources, wealth, and overall estate are to be distributed is critical. As a pastor, I always encouraged folks to set up a plan for the distribution of their assets, with periodic modifications. I would bring in an expert to hold a seminar. This proved most helpful and was ever a means of relieving tension and anxiety for those who had never taken that step. As early as possible, people should decide how the distribution should be made. Countless millions of dollars annually fill state coffers because assets were not distributed under a legal last will and testament.[25]

One of the most difficult steps in making the transition from being a parent's child to being a parent's parent is sitting down with the parents and discussing their finances. Even if not well versed in the world of finance, read up on it and then bring in someone who is an expert in the field.

> After a frank and open discussion of all of the parents' goals and objectives, you and your parents may begin to recognize the areas that need attention. After you and your parents have gathered all of the pertinent information, together, you will identify other areas of concern. You will also proceed to implement changes with considerable assurance that your parents will be responsive to the changes, since they have participated in the discovery process and understand that the changes are necessary to meet specific goals or shortfalls which they have identified.[26]

Oddly enough, just when the sandwich generation begins to feel the pressure of helping an elderly parent(s), there is evidence to show that the elderly are the ones just as often assisting the adult child(ren) financially. In a 1975 Louis Harris poll, the findings showed that 45 percent of the public aged sixty-five and older help their children and grandchildren with money, recognizing that aging parents generally do not wish to draw on their children's financial resources.[25] Though the government is being pressured to provide more and more for the elderly, studies show that families prefer to take care of their own.

> Evidence on norms of intergenerational economic obligations is mixed. On the one hand, Americans believe in familial economic support. Two-thirds of family heads in 1960 felt that relatives should be responsible for old people in need. When asked about their preferences for family versus non family assistance (financial and other forms), a random sample of 450 respondents voiced preference for family, regardless of age, cohort, gender, education, and marital status. In another study, respondents aged seventy-two and older, those widowed or divorced, those with low incomes, and those in poor health had greater expectations of support from their children. These studies suggest both a preference for family support and general norms of family economic obligations, although they may be situationally defined by need. On the other hand, there is evidence that economic support of adults—at least older adults—is seen as the responsibility

of the state rather than the family. In 1974, 96 percent of the public agreed that the government should provide income for older people when they are no longer working. Fully 91 percent of adult children in one sample saw their parents as having no need for "income services" from them, and 45 percent of the children expected regular government income assistance for their parents in the future.[28]

All of this financial concern, of course, begs the question: What do I do to care for the financial future of not just my aging parents, but my immediate family, too? Consider the following information provided in an article by MFS Investment Management, a mutual fund company. According to a survey performed for MFS by the Roper Starch Worldwide polling organization, the majority of Americans ages 40-64 are concerned about such financial issues as providing aid to adult children and estate planning but fewer than half are taking the essential steps to address those concerns. Despite the lack of action, 59 percent say they are concerned that their children "will need help from them in their 20s and beyond" and 40 percent say they are concerned about being able to help their aging parents face a range of financial issues.[29]

MEDICAL INSURANCE

In today's high cost of living and even higher cost of adequate medical care, a sound plan and investment into a medical insurance policy is no longer a luxury, it is essential. Some would even say it is a right. Life savings quickly disappear in today's hospitals loaded with the latest high-tech equipment and experts in all areas of medical practice. In fact, financial ruin for the individual and the extended family is not uncommon. Many today are calling on our government to implement socialized medicine in order to make prevention and treatment affordable and available for all. It is not the intent of this book to debate the pros and cons of socialized medicine. However, it does highlight the dilemma that many people are in today who are just not able to receive adequate medical care. Families need to work out a course of action prior to the need for hospitalization and treatment. It needs to be a course of action that they can live with and where they are not caught by surprise. Once again, doing some research in this area, sitting down with elderly parents, and charting a course will remove much fear and anxiety. Jamia Jasper Jacobsen walks the reader through a knowledgeable understanding of these phases in medical care and coverage.

PHYSICAL FITNESS

Americans are frequently accused of being overweight compared to other societies in the world. If the interest in fitness clubs, video tapes and diet plans is any indicator, then there must be some truth to this. But what about our seniors? Does it matter whether the elderly stay in shape? Should it matter? Why not just grow old and enjoy a time of rest and ease? Many researchers and studies suggest quite strongly that the benefits of regular exercise are unquestioned.

Al Brenda is the owner of several fitness centers, one of which is located in my town. Al is 69 and is in terrific shape. He competes in the Masters Track and Field and has won numerous events. During the past thirty years he has been a four-time Senior Olympic Decathlon Champion ('76-'79), two-time National Master's Decathlon ('78 & '82), third in the World Master's Pentathlon ('83), second in the Pole Vault of the World Championships ('85), World Decathlon Champion ('82), National Indoor Pentathlon Champion ('90), and National Pole Vault Champion ('92).

It goes back to his boyhood days in Dearborn, Michigan when a school coach gave all the kids an opportunity to try various track and field events. He took to it naturally and hasn't looked back. He says at that point he realized he had a gift from God in athletics. "And I've tried to use that gift,"[30] he said. He coached football for 36 years on the high school and college levels.

Citing the research performed in the Framingham (Massachusetts) Study and the Harvard Study on Geriatrics, Al says everyone can make some improvement in their overall physical condition. Of course, a medical doctor should be consulted prior to attempting anything remotely strenuous, he adds. One study showed terrific results in people in their 70's to 90's who were bedridden. They were encouraged to use very light dumbbells and do curls. The improvements were most noticeable in the blood circulation and flexibility, positively affecting the person's overall health. He strongly recommends that if an individual has been sedentary for some time, they should get in touch with a physical fitness expert who will thoroughly check them out and write a plan of training to be followed.

One of the reasons so many people feel physically bad in their later years is the lack of exercise. Exercise, Al says, removes the toxin buildup in the body. What other benefits are there? The obvious health benefits, of course, particularly in the cardiovascular area, and in muscle fitness. It's important to understand, Al says, that muscle fitness is not merely toning the muscles. It is lifting weights, "really pumping iron," and making the body respond to the exercise plan. "The Arizona State Research Studies, as far back as fifteen years ago, pointed out that one who just pumps iron . . . , contrary to what was believed for decades . . . , who pumps iron, who is a muscle head, they found out that person can be almost as cardiovascularly [sic] fit pumping iron in an intelligent, educated way . . . , their blood pressure, shockingly, came down!"[31]

A way to get started in your fitness plan is to involve yourself slowly at first with light walking/jogging. Al uses a metaphor of a baby needing to crawl before it can walk. So it is true for the person starting out either for the first time, or after a long absence, in an effort to get back into physical shape. He advises the people to at first only come to the club twice a week for three to four weeks. This way you don't burn yourself out. Then gradually increase your attendance. He further recommends becoming involved in athletic programs sponsored by schools, churches, and community athletic programs. Look to age-group competition. Al believes the weight training is essential to avoid the common injuries and maladies that many people experience when strictly running. The muscle development, including tendons and ligaments, act as "shock absorbers" when properly exercised, reducing the breakdown of cartilage. This is why aquarobics is so helpful.

"When you're 50-55 and you want to get back into a fitness program, you have to think nutritionally,"[32] Al says. He points out the fact that the body does not assimilate foods as rapidly or in as large a quantity as it did when you were sixteen. He suggests drinking juices you make yourself with a good brand of juicer. His favorite is carrots and green apples. I tried it and it's not too bad! He refers to the story of Daniel and his friends in the Bible who refused to eat the foods offered by the king. Daniel said, "'Please test us for ten days: Give us nothing but vegetables to eat and water to drink. Then compare our appearance with that of the young men who eat the royal food . . .' At the end of ten days they looked healthier and better nourished," (Daniel 1:12, 13 & 15).

You may not be at the level of a world class athlete like Al. Or even Bobbie Thomas, the 1996 state and national champion in the 100, 200 and 400 meter race and who has not lost a race since in his age group, 60-64. Thomas is not satisfied, however, to sit back and rest on his laurels.

> "When you are the fastest in the world, why slow down?" asks Thomas. He trains at Sacramento [Calif.] State University five days a week between 4:00 and 5:30 p.m. He warms up by jogging 800 meters and also goes through stretching and running drills. "I have about one dozen seniors coming and working out with me," said Thomas. "I'm trying to stimulate them to be active. They are competing now, too."[33]

Several times a week I play handball with my friend Bill Greenaway, a 72-year-old, who is in superb condition. I'm nearly a quarter of a century younger and it's all I can do to win a game against him. Personally, I've always loved sports and as a former Marine, staying in shape is a way of life for me. I continue to lift weights, jog, play handball and racquetball, so I love to see someone enjoy physical exercise the way Bill does, refusing to give in to the aging process. Bill recently teamed up with a longtime friend, a retired Air Force general who is now 60, for a game of doubles against Bill's two forty-something sons. They played five games straight with Bill and the general winning the last game. Bill was heard to say, "I just hope I can keep doing this."

My stepfather and grandmother were advocates of keeping fit through exercise. My grandmother still walked a mile a day at a brisk clip up until she was 91. My stepfather walked a mile or two every day on top of playing several rounds of golf each week up until his death at 80. Notably, they had far fewer physical problems than many of their age.

Studies have shown that even a very mild amount of exercise for those who have never been active increases blood circulation (a problem often experienced by the elderly), reduces the pain and discomfort of arthritis, and generally improves a person's outlook and sense of well-being. In an article entitled "Reverse the Brain Drain," by R. Daniel Foster in *Cooking Light*, he reports that clinical and laboratory research suggests that regular physical exercise makes the body more adept at delivering essential oxygen and nutrients to the brain.

Your brain is a hungry machine that makes up just 2% of your body weight but consumes 20% of your total oxygen and glucose stores. It operates best when nutrient-delivering channels like arteries are kept clear -- which is exactly what happens when you exercise. In fact, exercise has been shown to promote new capillary growth in the brains of rats that hit the treadmill regularly. Those new capillaries feed nerve cells and help impulses travel faster across the gaps between nerve endings.[34]

Any exercise is a plus. Foster says even moderate exercise can be good for the brain. One study showed a group that walked 50 minutes three times a week for four months not only boosted their cardiovascular fitness level by 27%, but also excelled in cognitive measures compared to a sedentary group. Other research indicates that older sedentary types can start reversing brain drain with exercise, even after years of inactivity.[35]

Physical fitness should be part of everyone's daily activities. By staying fit, the elderly person, in particular, is far less likely to be a burden on their family and friends. The mentally and physically fit person enjoys a great deal more independence as they move into their later years.

NOTES

1. Gary R. Collins, *Christian Counseling: A Comprehensive Guide*, rev. ed. (Dallas: Word Publishing, 1988), 203.

2. Miriam Baker Nye, *But I Never Thought He'd Die* (Philadelphia: Westminister Press, 1978), 14-15.

3. Jamia Jasper Jacobsen, "Aging America," in *Help! I'm Parenting My Parents*, ed. (Indianapolis: Benchmark Press, 1988), 7-8.

4. Dubbie Hoffman Buckler, "The Problem of Elder Abuse and Neglect," in *Help! I'm Parenting My Parents*, ed. Jamia Jasper Jacobsen (Indianapolis: Benchmark Press, 1988), 240.

5. "Caught in the Middle: Use Home Caregivers to Relieve 'Sandwich Generation' Stress," *Kelly Assisted Living (KAL) Press Releases*, http://www.kellyservices.com/kal/pressrel/kalnews08.html, October 1996.

6. Don Anderson, *Keep the Fire!* (Sisters, Oreg.: Multnomah Books, 1994), 11.

7. E. Robert Edwards, "Substance Abuse in Older Parents," in *Help! I'm Parenting My Parents*, ed. Jamia Jasper Jacobsen (Indianapolis: Benchmark Press, 1988), 205.

8. Ibid.

9. Allen J. Moore, "The Family Relations of Older Persons," in *Ministry with the Aging,* ed. William M. Clements (New York: Haworth Press, 1989), 179.

10. Jacobsen, ed., introduction to *Help! I'm Parenting My Parents*, 4.

11. Ken Dychtwald, *Age Wave* (Los Angeles: J. P. Tarcher, 1989), 240-41.

12. Ibid., 238.

13. Irene Goldenberg and Herbert Goldenberg, *Family Therapy: An Overview*, 2nd ed. (Pacific Grove, Calif: Brooks/Cole Publishing, 1985), 16.

14. David K. Switzer, *Pastoral Care Emergencies: Ministering to People in Crisis,* (New York: Paulist Press, 1989), 148.

15. Ibid., 17.

16. Ibid., 18

17. Ibid.

18. "Between Old & Young," Brooks Clark, *Aging Parents,* http://www.metropulse.com/dir_zine/cover_dir/619_aging.html, 1997.

19. David H. Olson, et al., *Prepare/Enrich Counselor's Manual* (Minneapolis: Life Innovations, 1992), 110; and *Taylor-Johnson Temperament Analysis* (Thousand Oaks, Calif.: Psychological Publications, n.d.).

20. Dychtwald, 242.

21. Pauline K. Regan, *Aging Parents* (Los Angeles: University of Southern California, Ethel Percey Andrews Gerontology Center, 1979), 62-63.

22. James W. Ewing, "Adults with Parents Crisis: A Personal Account," in *Ministry with the Aging*, ed. William M. Clements (New York: Haworth Press, 1989), 203.

23. Jacobsen, 35.

24. Ibid., 36.

25. Ibid., 36-37.

26. Ibid., 37.

27. Jay A. Mancini, *Aging Parents and Adult Children* (Lexington, Mass;, Lexington Books, 1989), 183.

28. Ibid., 183-84.

29. "National Survey Finds Majority of Affluent 'Sandwich Generation' Americans Fail to do Financial Planning for Adult Children, Aging Parents," *MFS Mutual Funds Online*, http://www.mfs.com/about/news/press_080296.html, 1997.

30. Personal interview with Al Brenda, July 29, 1997.

31. Ibid.

32. Ibid.

33. Hilda Bloomquist, "Make Way for the BT Express," *Today's Senior Magazine*, May 1997, 14.

34. R. Daniel Foster, "Reverse the Brain Drain," *Cooking Light*, 1996, 54.

35. Ibid., 56.

III
Willing and Able:
Who's Responsible for Whom?

Most families are very willing to assist elderly family members in whatever way possible. Yet how many of those same family members are really able to assist? The cost is more than financial. The emotions are seriously stretched during times when an elder parent is going through a crisis.

Perhaps it is this very predicament that many families find themselves in when they must seriously evaluate who cares for whom. Do elderly parents want assistance from their children? How much help? And what kind? These situations often arise just when a family has reached mid-life, with the children out on their own, or soon to be. Free-time and finances are loosened, and Bingo! an aging parent needs assistance.

ETHNIC AND MINORITY CULTURES

There is a commonly held belief that certain ethnic cultures take better care of their aging generations than might be found as a whole in western cultures. The facts from research indicate this is not true. It is even believed by many that Americans used to take better care of their elderly.

Americans distort history and create myth. Vivian's mother speaks longingly about a time and place when children looked after and loved

25

their parents. Although most people cherish this belief, it is a myth that
evokes anger and hurt from aged parents and guilt and despair from
children. . . . One researcher argued that there is no culture where old
people are loved and revered simply for being old, and no historical
time when children looked after and lived with their aged parents out
of fondness alone. The source of disappointment for Vivian's mother
is more than personal; we can trace it to a myth that pervades
American people. There are many such cultural myths, metaphors, and
contradictions that shape personal responsibility between aged parents
and their children. Responsibility is a suppressed ethic in American
culture. People talk about their family ties in the language of
economics, and freedom from interference, rather than responsibility,
is the most deeply held moral ground. Vivian says 'love has to be
earned' even by mothers and sons. Several scholars have traced these
economic and individualistic understandings of self and relationship to
liberal capitalism. The individualism that dominates public life is
reproduced in private life.[1]

LEGISLATIVE PRESSURE

As people live longer, there is increased pressure on the government to
provide adequate care and facilities for the elderly. So organized has this
segment of our population become that groups like the Gray Panthers
have exerted strong lobbying pressure on Congress to enact legislation
for the elderly. Recognizing that a person's family cannot do everything
for the elderly family member, it then becomes imperative to know what
agencies have been set up to assist in the care of the loved one [See
Appendix A].

In the election furor of 1994, the Republicans in the House of
Representatives created a *Contract with America*. Of the ten major issues
in the contract one issue pertains to helping senior citizens.

Proposals would raise the Social Security earnings limit which
currently pushes seniors out of the work force, eventually elevating the
limit to $30,000 by the year 2000. The *Senior Citizens Act would
repeal 1993 tax hikes on benefits* [italics in original], and provide tax

incentives for private, long-term-care insurance to let older Americans keep more of what they have earned.[2]

If the new congress is able to enact legislation that would allow senior citizens to make more money without losing their social security benefits then this would help take the burden off of families in providing care-giver services. Obviously the health of the elderly person would need to be considered, but many of the elderly are still very capable of doing a full day's work. In fact, there is expressed resentment by some that they have been "put out to pasture." Though they enjoy retirement for a time, they often become frustrated in being non-productive after spending their entire lives being very productive. Often this desire to contribute is to the advantage of the church where there are numerous opportunities to be useful. This involvement of the elderly in the life of the church is addressed in Chapter 6.

Perhaps the best solution for the present elder care situation is a combination of both family and government resources. There is plenty of evidence to support the family being the best source of assistance for the elder family member. "Americans agree that kin have some general obligations, but they accept the government's role and do not, in practice, expect to have to help out financially. Indeed, independence is valued."[3] Following the independence theme, Mancini's book *Aging Parents and Adult Children* concludes that "while Americans accept the notion of financial assistance from the state, other kinds of support are still viewed as the province of the family. For example, family members are preferred over formal service providers when it comes to financial management, food shopping, and confidences.[4]

THE CAREGIVER: ALWAYS ON CALL

The sandwich generation finds itself in the unenviable position of being caregivers to family members who, for varying reasons, are in need of assistance. When the elderly arrive at retirement they never intend to have others ever be in the position of having to take care of them. With some money put away in the bank, Social Security, and maybe a little work on the side, the now retired person is ready to relax and enjoy life. "The last fifth of life is reduced to a recreational interlude before the sweet by and by,"[5] can be heard from various quarters. The operative word is "they never intend." Lyric Wallwork Winik writes about Garth Hartley and the difficulties he encountered when finding himself suddenly burdened with the responsibility of taking care of both parents. "It wasn't supposed to be this way," he said. "For my wife, Kathy, and myself, this changed the way we lived. I was not prepared for this, but I just wanted to try to protect these folks, my parents."[6] Now, Hartley, and countless others, find themselves caring for their aging parents. "As a caregiver, one of the best things you can do for the patient is to take care of yourself," says Lisa Gabel, geriatric social worker at the Moses H. Cone Geriatric Assessment Center.[7]

Peggy Matthews, Director of Women's Education Center at the Women's Hospital, Washington, D.C. says, "A person who is dealing with the kind of stress that comes with constant caregiving needs an outlet." According to the National Council on Aging (NCOA), most caregivers at some point feel tired, isolated, helpless, angry, resentful, and then guilty for having these negative feelings. While it's natural to have these feelings, the council explained, it's also important not to keep everything bottled up inside.[8]

For many who are on the threshold of retirement, they find themselves in a major predicament. They have not planned adequately for either their final years, or they anticipated being able to work as long as they wanted. The average worker today has forty years to make enough money to survive 10, 15 or more years of retirement. The Social Security Administration offers the following sobering statistics.

Out of 100 people at age 65:

- 34 are dead
- 54 are dead broke
- 5 are still working
- 4 are financially independent
- 1 is wealthy[9]

The failure to adequately plan for the retirement years automatically casts the oversight and care of the elderly person on someone—that someone initially being immediate family. "It is reported that 93 percent of the men at age 65 who have failed financially said it was because of a lack of a plan."[10]

The reality of the situation gets worse. People are just not aware of what is needed to survive beyond sixty-five. Almost half of American households have no plan at all for retirement. This is one reason many companies are requiring their employees to invest in an IRA. Some companies go so far as to automatically take it out of the workers pay.

> Today's workers aren't likely to retire in style—and may not be able to retire at all. . . . Nearly eight out of 10 households will have less than half the income they need to be comfortable in retirement. . . . Even households with pension plans are likely to have only 50 to 60 percent of the income they need in retirement.[11]

Statistics pertaining to the elderly and the ages they reach are staggering.

> The "graying of America" is increasingly visible. One of every eight adults is over age 65. The fastest growing segment of our population is over age 85. Many senior adults in our communities and congregations reach the golden years only to find those years tarnished by illness, insufficient income, separation from family, and the loss of spouse and friends. [T]hey carry heavy loads of past hurts into the latter years. No wonder some seniors prefer to tune out of life and retreat into memories of the glory days (Job 29:4) when God's favor was felt more clearly (Psalm 77:5-12).[12]

According to one gerontologist, the post retirement years are divided into four categories: the Young Old (60 to 69), the Middle-Aged Old (70 to 79), the Old-Old (80 to 89) and the Very Old-Old (90 to 99). With the increasing longevity in the United States, the adult life expectancy is 17.3 years greater than the traditional retirement age of 65.[13]

Enter, the caregiver. This individual is more than likely to be a female adult child of the elderly person, or a daughter-in-law of the elderly person. It has been reported that the average woman spends seventeen years raising her children and eighteen years caring for elderly parents (either hers or her husbands). But the primary caregiver is the spouse, followed by adult children. Yet often the spouse is in no condition to care for an aging/ailing mate. A sense of helplessness pervades the elderly couple, creating a fear of what may lie ahead for them. In a recent conversation, one woman told me of the deterioration process her parents went through in their advancing age. The father had to be admitted to a nursing home as he was in the latter stages of Alzheimer's disease. While leaving the nursing facility, the mother commented aloud that she never wanted to be placed in such a place. Her fear was that she would wind up in the same condition as her husband. Today, she resides in a nursing home, having lost all her faculties as Alzheimer's claimed yet another victim.

> About 20 percent of older Americans need help getting out of bed and bathing. Millions more need help with finances, meals and transportation. Overwhelmingly, it is their families who provide that help—only about 5 percent of elderly Americans live in nursing homes.[14]

Studies have shown that women of differing socioeconomic backgrounds perform their tasks of caregiving in different ways.

> Women from higher socioeconomic backgrounds frequently assume a "care-manager" role, where they identify needed services and manage their provision, often by formal service providers. Lower socioeconomic class women are more likely to be "care-providers," performing the care tasks themselves.[15]

Caregivers often pay a price for providing assistance to the elderly parent. "The emotional burdens of feeling alone, isolated, and without time for oneself appear to be the greatest costs."[16] So who cares for the caregiver? In recent years attempts have been made to offer training, support and encouragement to caregivers through several organizations nationwide. Self-help groups have appeared with names like "Children with Aging Parents," "You and Your Aging Parents," and "Generations."[17] Diane Labonte, a Warren Shepell counselor in

Montreal, sees many sandwich generation clients who feel "stretched to the limit." She has noticed that as stress and problems mount, health may be affected. Labonte has noticed that overburdened caregivers tend to experience frequent colds, migraines and back problems.[18]

A bright spot in the caregiving arena comes from sociologist Gary Lee of the Social Research Center of Washington State University. He says, "As a category, the American elderly are afflicted by many social and personal problems. Collective neglect by their families is not one of them."[19] Perhaps this is why statistics from the U.S. Senate show that adult children and spouses provide more than one-third of elder care. Seventy percent of caregivers were women; 74 percent of caregivers live with the recipient; and 64 percent had provided care for at least a year.[20]

One possible option for the caregiver who is taking care of the elderly parent full-time is to consider investing in an ECHO House. ECHO stands for Elder Cottage Housing Opportunity, also known as "Granny flats." These houses originated in Australia and have begun making inroads in the United States.

> It works like this: you think your aging mother, grandfather, or friend might be more comfortable, better cared for, and less lonesome if he or she lived close enough for you to keep an eye out, to visit, or to take over a hot meal. But your home is too small, or your family is unwilling to accommodate such an arrangement. Call the local ECHO company, and within hours they'll come by with a truck and place a lovely cottage in your backyard, complete with a bedroom, living room, bathroom, utility nook, and kitchen. The cottage has a heating system and a stacked washer and dryer. Your "significant elder" has privacy and can come and go as he or she pleases, but is only steps away if the kids want to drop by and visit, if there's any problem, or if he or she wants to join you for dinner.[21]

This sounds like an excellent idea, but only for those who can afford the investment of fifteen to twenty thousand dollars, and who have the necessary acreage.

One group of Americans has been taking care of their elderly along these lines for centuries. They are the Amish. The ECHO houses are very

popular with the Amish who have traditionally built what they call
Grossmutter (grandmother) houses on their farms.[22]

There is a multiplex retirement community for older Americans in
Turlock, California. The primary retirement facility is called Covenant
Village, with companion facilities to take care of the elderly who are in
varying degrees of physical and/or mental deterioration. All facilities are
located across the street from Emanuel Medical Center, the primary
hospital in town. Recent residents of Covenant Village shared some
interesting perspectives in a newspaper article.

> Covenant Village offers nonmedical assisted living for those who need
> some help. It also contracts with Brandel Manor for skilled nursing
> care and with Emanuel Medical Center for acute care. . . . That's one
> of the reasons the Brydon's were attracted to Covenant Village. Many
> of their friends and family didn't understand why they wanted to come
> to a retirement home. "I don't think they realized how much
> responsibility it is to take care of parents," Andy Brydon said. "We did
> not want to be dependent on our children," Margaret Brydon said.[23]

The caregiver is always in a precarious position since there are no
certainties of what level of care will be required. Always in the back of
the mind is the concern of "What if. . . .?" What if mom requires
expensive surgery not covered by insurance? What if dad begins to
behave irrationally, exhibiting the early stages of Alzheimer's? What if
my own resources just aren't enough to assist my aging parents? These
and many other questions periodically plague the sandwich generation
caregiver [See Appendix C].

There are some options to be considered by the caregiver that may
just help the situation. One option is an assisted-living program,
available at some retirement homes, where residents live in small
apartments but receive meals and limited care.[24] Another option is an
adult day-care program.

> There are nearly 3000 adult day-care programs nationwide, where the
> elderly are supervised, with meals provided and even medication
> administered. "It is designed to help people stay in their homes and to
> help family members care for them as long as possible," explained Jill

Glassman, assistant director of Somerset County's Adult Day Center in Bridgewater, N.J.[25]

The directors at the Horizon Nursing Daycare, Trenton, New Jersey, have three site objectives in approaching long-term health care. They are sold on adult (nursing) day care service as the only service that currently makes sense. The site objectives are:

To help senior citizens and caregivers consider every alternative when choosing long-term care.

To provide a comprehensive source of educational materials and insights on the subjects of adult day care, home health care and long-term care for consumers and health care professionals.

To promote adult day care as the first choice in the continuum of care due to its desirability, depth of services and economic feasibility.[26]

Yet another option is an adult foster-care program. In this program, which originated in Oregon, older adults who are unable to live on their own can move into the home of a specially trained and licensed foster-care provider for far less than the cost of a nursing home.[27]

For employers, the issue of employees feeling the need to care for aging parents can create additional stresses, both for the employee and the employer. An article from the Internet entitled, "Assist the Sandwich Generation With Their Parents," is aimed directly at the problem faced by employers and how they can help their "sandwiched" employees.

Many employees are members of the sandwich generation, with children in school or day care and older relatives in elder care. This creates extraordinary stress on the workers, but also on the workers' children. An estimated one-third of the work force bears caregiving responsibility for older relatives; about half of those relatives are located more than 100 miles away. Some businesses are realizing that their employees and their productivity are suffering from the anxiety and hours away from work required to care for the elderly. Employees fear they will be accused of caring more for their families than their jobs and see their role as caregiver to older relatives as carrying the same stigma single parents feel.

Help employees care for elders.

Several businesses, including IBM, offer resource and referral services, including telephone networks for counseling, information about services in the elder's community, and screened referrals. IBM offered the first nationwide elder care referral service; several other companies now do the same. Others tap into local referral services.

Include elder care in tax-deductible benefits.

Some companies are offering pre-tax programs similar to those used for day care to help cover the cost of elder care.

Provide subsidies for elder care.

Travelers in Hartford, Connecticut, gives employees direct subsidies of $400 to $1200 a year for elder care. First Hawaiian, a Honolulu bank, offers an elder-care subsidy of as much as $200 a month, an aid in retaining workers in the city's tight labor market. Some companies offer elder-care subsidies as part of their flexible benefit packages.

Offer long-term insurance.

Another optional benefit gaining in popularity is long-term care insurance to help cover the cost of nursing home care; the insurance is usually available for both spouses and their parents.

Make company day-care centers intergenerational.

Stride Rite opened the first intergenerational company day-care center in the nation in 1990, after surveying employees and finding that 25 percent were caring for older relatives and another 13 percent were expected to take on caregiving roles for the elderly in the next five years. The center has space for 55 children and 24 elders, with separate and common areas located in the company's office tower. The program is open to the elderly in the community, as well as those related to employees, and it allows them to be part of their children's lives.[28]

Some recent studies are indicating that caring for aging parents by the sandwich generation is not as dreadful as it might first seem. Many are saying that there are many benefits that come from providing physical, emotional, even financial assistance to loved ones in need. More and more researchers, including sociologist Dr. Vicki Lamb of the University of South Carolina, are beginning to use favorable terms to describe life in the sandwich generation.

"I don't think that women with children and parents are having a day-to-day care-giving dilemma," says Lamb, who studies the trends of health and aging. "Most elderly today are not excessively disabled and don't require constant supervision. The family is still the first line of defense for any caregiving, but that doesn't mean it is a one-sided relationship. There is reciprocity between generations that can be very positive."

Most sandwich generation stories aren't as grim and stressful as people are made to believe, Lamb says. Those who care for seriously disabled parents and juggle multiple responsibilities are a minority and shouldn't define the age group.

"There are many positives. Giving back to a parent can be very satisfying," says Lamb. "Parents are not passive recipients of care; they can provide continued advice and emotional support to their adult children."[29]

An interesting trend is taking place in the last half of the 1990's. The caregivers who are shouldering the responsibility of the aging are not just family members and health professionals, but neighbors, friends, clubs, and churches.

A decade ago surveys showed that 7 million American households included individuals who were taking care of somebody else; today that number is more than 22.4 million, according to Gail Hunt, executive director of the National Alliance for Caregiving. "They're caring not just for relatives, but for neighbors and friends," she says. "And not just helping with grocery shopping, but actually helping with more personal concerns."

According to recent Census Bureau data, more people in need of assistance are counting on unpaid nonrelatives than they are on hired helpers like nurse's aides or companions.

"Eight out of ten people say they want to live out their lives at home - and that wouldn't be possible without help from volunteers and neighbors," says health-care activist Roger McFarlane, author of *The*

36 The Sandwich Generation

Complete Bedside Companion: No-Nonsense Advice on Caring for the Seriously Ill (Simon & Schuster, due out in late fall).

"Increasingly, there's a neighbor, a Kiwanis Club member, a friend from church, a lover, or even the relative of a friend - ordinary Americans who are stepping in to help in a big way," he says. "There are monumental, historical trends at work here."

Frequently, the helpful neighbor who keeps tabs on an older person is another older citizen. According to a just-released national survey sponsored by the National Alliance for Caregiving and AARP, 12.4 percent of those who look out for older people are themselves 65 or older.[30]

SANDWICHED SENSITIVITY:
A SENSE OF HUMOR HELPS

The current attitude in American society toward the elderly is troubling at best. With our nation becoming an increasingly older population, the attitudes expressed through the media are a bit unnerving. If you are young, beautiful/handsome, a jet-setter, then all is well. If you are old, slow, and no longer (if ever) beautiful or handsome, you are a nonentity. By implication, you are not important; you are not to be taken seriously; you are a leech on society; you are troublesome, obstinate, and often meddlesome; you are in the way; and you are a target for the disreputable in society. On top of all that, you are the object of many jokes and tricks.

Ageism abounds in the advertising world. Aging is marketed as negative, undesirable, useless, and even avoidable. Few of us will do what national marketing executive Pat Moore did—dressed, made-up, and lived as an 80-year-old woman in different cities—but we can certainly appreciate her experiences. The marketplace itself avoids the aging person. Aging looks are to be avoided in make-up and dress and "old age illnesses and senility" are to be avoided as a fate equal to death. Just look at the line of party goods and cards marketed to see who bears the brunt of our "humor."[31]

Nancy Datan writes that the humor of aging serves both intrapsychic and social-structural purposes. Humor by and about old people can be seen to deflect the painful truths of biological decline and inevitable death and thus, as Freud suggested, to convert the unbearable into the humorous—and so to master, in the mind at least, that which eventually will prove to master us.[32] Datan goes on to suggest that the social use of humor is a two-edged sword. For the younger set, it has a way of creating a distance from the older set, and the humor is thus often cruel and hurtful. It may be compared to any other form of humor that seeks to elevate one group while putting down another. The older generation uses humor to better face their aging predicament, strengthening their resolve to see themselves, and possibly others, through this final phase of life just as they survived every other phase of life. To express and exercise humor in this manner is to still maintain some power in life. One senior citizen lamented, "People compliment me on my youthful appearance. They never said a word when I still had it."[33] To be able to look at yourself and laugh is indeed healthy. My father often said to me while I was growing up, and prone to seeing things with sober-sidedness, "Don't take yourself so seriously!" Right up to his death at 80 years of age, he practiced that philosophy.

The late Erma Bombeck wrote some of the most humorous articles about aging that I have yet to run across. In one article entitled, "Rats Prove Aging Doesn't Make Folks No-brainers," she cited her theories on the aging process.

Somewhere in the decade of your 20s, your eyes will go. No one wants to admit this, but when you see someone in a restaurant drop a menu on the floor, stare at it then say, "I'll have spinach tortellini and a house salad," you begin to suspect his vision is not as good as it used to be.

Knees and feet emerge as the No. 1 topic of conversation in the 30s. That's when old football wounds reappear, tennis serves slow down, and you can't pass a chair without sitting in it. More and more people appear at social functions wearing tennis shoes and explaining they're having foot problems.

All the backs go in the 40s. It's an epidemic. Either someone has a bad back, is getting a bad back, or has advice on how to get rid of a bad back. The person always begins the conversation by saying, "Man was never meant to walk upright."

The mind begins to fail you in the 50s. You can't find your car in the mall and you can't remember if you added salt to the potatoes. You not only cannot recall the punch line, you can't remember the joke.

Sex. It's somewhere in the first five. Where it is on the list depends on how serious the first four are.[34]

To laugh at oneself is healthy. To be laughed at is not. Only those who are in old age can fully appreciate being old. They were, after all, young once themselves, so they know what that phase of life is all about. But the young cannot truly appreciate old age until they themselves are old. Consider this humorous letter.

Remember, old folks are worth a fortune - silver in their hair, gold in their teeth, stones in their kidneys, lead in their feet, and gas in their stomachs.

I have become a little older since I saw you last, and a few changes have come into my life since then. Frankly, I have become quite a frivolous old gal. I am seeing five gentlemen every day.

As soon as I wake up, Will Power helps me get out of bed. Then I go see John. Then Charlie Horse comes along, and when he is here he takes a lot of my time and attention. When he leaves Arthur Ritis shows up and stays the rest of the day. He doesn't like to stay in place very long, so he takes me from joint to joint. After such a busy day I'm really tired and glad to go to bed with Ben Gay. What a life!

P.S. The preacher came to call the other day. He said at my age I should be thinking about the hereafter. I told him, "Oh, I do all the time. No matter where I am - in the parlor, upstairs, in the kitchen, or down in the basement - I ask myself what am I here after?[35]

Sensitivity is critical when interacting with elderly parents. Keeping a sense of humor, enjoying reminiscences, and creating new experiences are all integral for maintaining a healthy environment for both the elderly parent(s) and the adult child (see Chapter 7, "LifeStories"). Reaffirm the older person's place in the family structure, being careful not to take away anymore responsibilities than is necessary. The fact that you may find yourself becoming your parents parent does not presuppose that you are to treat them like children. Respect their wishes and desires. You, too, will be old one day.

The following poem is a modern, light-hearted look at the way many older Americans are facing the future. Perhaps you know someone like this!

OUR COMPUTER-AGE GRANDMA

The old rocking chair is empty today,
For grandma is no longer in it.
She's off in her car to her office or shop,
And buzzing around every minute.

No one shoves grandma back on the shelf,
She's versatile, forceful, dynamic.
That isn't a pie in the oven, my dear.
Her baking today is ceramics.

You won't see her trudging early to bed,
From her place in the warm chimney nook.
Her computer clickety-clacks through the night,
For grandma is writing a book.

Grandmother never takes one backward look,
To slow down her steady advancing.
She won't tend the babies for you anymore,
For grandma has taken up line-dancing.

She isn't content with the crumbs of old thoughts,
With meager and second-hand knowledge.
Don't bring your mending to grandma to do,
Grandma has gone back to college![36]

NOTES

1. Mancini, 265.
2. From NAE *Insight*, vol. 17, no. 2, Church Edition (Washington, D.C.: NAE Office of Public Affairs, Feb. 1995).
3. Mancini, 184.
4. Ibid., 192.

5. Anderson, 36.

6. Lyric Wallwork Winik, "How Much Can I Give?" *Parade, Modesto* [Calif.] *Bee*, 29 Jan. 1995, 4.

7. "Caring for the Caregiver Often Neglected," *Caregiver Network*, Women's Health Matters, http://www.caregiver.on.ca.caring-article.html; Winter 1995.

8. Ibid.

9. Steve Blumenthal, interview with the author, a financial investor with Blumenthal & Associates, Salinas, Calif., 22 Oct. 1994.

10. Ibid.

11. Ibid.

12. Kathie Erwin, "Looking Backward, Looking Ahead—Helping Elders Cope," *Christian Counseling Today*, July 1993, 33.

13. Ibid.

14. Winik, 4.

15. Nancy R. Hooyman, and H. Asuman Kiyak, *Social Gerontology, A Multidisciplinary Perspective*, 2nd ed. (Boston: Allyn & Bacon, 1991), 309.

16. Ibid., 312.

17. Dychtwald, 249.

18. "The Sandwich Generation," Warren Shepell, *Bilan*, http://www.ocaq.qc.ca/bilan.96/bia12_4v.htm; July 1996.

19. Dychtwald, 240

20. Douglas C. Kimmel, *Adulthood and Aging*, 3rd ed. (New York: John Wiley & Sons, 1990), 493.

21. Dychtwald, 250.

22. Ibid., 250-51.

23. Valerie Wigglesworth, "Making the Move: Retirement Homes Today Cater to Active Living," *Turlock* [Calif.] *Journal*, 18 Jan. 1995, A5-6.

24. Winik, 6.

25. Ibid.

26. Jane R. Harkey, "Adult Day Care, A Sensible Solution," *Horizon Nursing Daycare*, Trenton, NJ, [http://home.algorithms.net/Horizon/frmain.htm] 19 Feb. 1997.

27. Winik, 6.

28. "Assist the Sandwich Generation With Their Parents," What you can do in your workplace, *Benton Foundation*, Washington, D.C., http://www.kidscampaigns.org/start/101workplace65.html; 1996.

29. "Sandwiched Boomers Don't Always Feel Squeezed, USC researcher says," *University of South Carolina*, Office of Media Relations,

http://uscnews.admin.scarolina.edu/uscnews/news/features/socy437.htm; December 3, 1996.

30. Joyce A. Post, "Caregivers: The New Compassion," *Modern Maturity*, May/June 1997, 74-75.

31. Buckler, 243.

32. Lucille Nahemow, Kathleen A. McCluskey-Fawcett, and Paul E. McGhee, eds., *Humor and Aging* (Orlando: Academic Press, 1986), 162.

33. Joe Drovdal, "Humor Chips," *Today's Senior Magazine*, Lodi, Calif., May 1997, 18.

34. Erma Bombeck, "Rats Prove Aging Doesn't Make Folks No-brainers," *Turlock* [Calif.] *Journal*, 26 Dec. 1994, A6.

35. Charles R. Swindoll, *Laugh Again*, (Dallas: Word Publishing, 1991), 211.

36. "Our Computer-Age Grandma," a poem, *Heritage House Herald*, Escalon, Calif., April 1997, 2.

IV

Honor Thy Father and Thy Mother:
An Ethical Paradox

The scriptures identify God as the author of marriage and the family (Genesis 2 and 3). Despite the problem of sin in humanity, God intended for this familial arrangement to be of great blessing and enjoyment for the human race. It often faces tough sledding in today's society, with pressures brought to bear on relationships that generations a few decades ago never imagined.

Yet the need for family to band together is wonderfully portrayed in the history of the Hebrew people as God faithfully saw them through incredible hardship and adversity. Blessings from an openhanded God were always forthcoming when the people walked in obedience. The same is true for the individual and family that places their faith and trust in the care of a covenantal God.

Though the individuals recorded in scripture often failed to walk faithfully with God, the same as people do today, the overriding message of holy scripture is that there is always hope.

Not only does a loving God seek to make a covenant relationship with fallen humanity, but the chance for transformation is always available as well as the window of opportunity that is given to walk away from a checkered past. Recognizing this fact, we will proceed to investigate a Christian understanding of parent/child relationships.

Tremendous ethical questions must be addressed from the teachings of scripture as to the role of honoring one's father and mother. The Christian teaching on this subject seems to have been followed without much deviation until the twentieth century. With the advent of higher technology, advanced medical practice, and the development of drugs that cure many diseases that were once deadly, the issues have changed. Just how do we interpret the scriptural teaching on taking care of our parents at a time in our history when they can literally be kept alive indefinitely through mechanical means and the administering of drugs? Should adult children be expected to parent their parents? How far does honoring one's parents go?

HONOR AND DISHONOR: THE ISSUE OF ABUSE

It is quite common for Christians to be confused when attempting to understand honor and the part it plays in their lives when taking care of the elderly. A closer look at the meaning of this word will serve to clear up the misunderstanding, and therefore the perpetuation of illogical and abusive relationships between adult children and their parents. In his book, *Family Ties Don't Have to Bind*, James Osterhaus presents valuable insight into the often stormy relations between generations because of a tradition of teaching that has historically jeopardized family cohesiveness instead of enhancing it. In chapter 2 under the section entitled, "Honoring Dishonorable Parents," he asks the question, "How should you go about honoring parents who have consistently dishonored you?" He lists four presuppositions for developing a framework in balancing honor of parents while keeping your own dignity and self-worth.

> First, you may have had a painful childhood, but that was not your responsibility. You are responsible for building a healthy life right now. There are connections between your childhood and your adult life, but those connections don't have to run—or ruin—your life in the present.
> Second, you are a separate person from your parents. You are entitled to think your own thoughts and feel your own feelings. You are an adult, and you are responsible for becoming your own person. Accepting that responsibility can be uncomfortable, but it is the key to overcoming the painful emotions, memories, and habits of the past.

Third, you are committed to looking honestly at your relationship with your parents. You are committed to uncovering and defusing the explosive secrets of the past. You refuse to let those secrets hurt you and control you any longer. You are committed to opening the lines of communication and reexamining the unspoken rules (such as "We don't talk about that," or "We don't acknowledge feelings"), you are committed to changing those rules and replacing denial with truth. As Jesus said, "And you shall know the truth, and the truth shall make you free."

Fourth, you are committed to confronting and dismantling any unhealthy control and power your parents may have held over your behavior or your feelings, whether they are living or dead. You can honor your parents even as you remove yourself from under their domination. You can honor your parents even as you confidently and fully assume the role of a self-reliant adult.[1]

Because child abuse has such devastating effects on the individual throughout their life with an array of ramifications, it is important to understand abuse as it takes place within society. I would postulate that those who have been abused as children are far more likely to be abusers of others later in life. That includes elderly parents who originally initiated the abuse.

One particular counseling case I had was with a woman who had been abused as a child. She revealed a combination of fear and hatred for the abuser, her father. If she could have done so she would have killed him. Yet she was still very much afraid of what he might do to her should her attempts fail, or if he even found out she considered such an action against him. Even as a grown woman she experienced physical abuse from him at family reunions and gatherings. She was afraid to attend these get-togethers, and she was afraid not to attend. Her fears prevented her from making any reports to the authorities. Thus, her cycle of fear continued. This has clearly had a detrimental effect on her own family and marriage.

It becomes apparent that many of our families are dysfunctional, showing little regard for offspring. It comes as no surprise therefore, when adult children often show a lack of interest and concern for elderly parents. However, as lamentable as the statistics are, the structure of the family unit should not be categorically dispatched, as some would suggest today.[2]

ELDER ABUSE

Tragically, the abuse of the elderly has been rising rapidly in our society. Perceived as weak and defenseless, often with no one around to look after them, the aging population in the United States is fearful of abuse. Elder abuse and neglect "constitutes inflicted harm or denied care."[3] There are four categories in defining elder abuse and neglect.

- *Physical Abuse* includes the willful hitting, slapping, beating, pushing, tripping, shoving, use of restraints/constraints, tying up, binding, sexually assaulting, and/or other methods of inflicting harm, pain, injury, or punishment to an indefensible elderly person.
- *Psychological Abuse* includes verbal assaults and threats, mental anguish, intimidation, humiliation, and/or the isolation of an elderly person.
- *Material, Fiduciary, or Financial Abuse* includes exercising unauthorized control over an elder's property or assets; stealing by deceiving, coercing, and/or otherwise taking advantage of an elderly person; and/or financially exploiting an elderly person through misuse of bank accounts, income, property, belongings, or other resources.
- *Neglect* includes the repeated failure of a care-giver to provide the basic necessities of life, including food, fluids, clothing, shelter, supervision, and medical care for an elderly person. Included in this category is self-neglect, a situation of inadvertent neglect as the elderly person fails to properly care for him/herself.[4]

Researchers have struggled with categorizing neglect. Due to the fact that neglect can be seen as covering a wide range of possibilities, certain researchers have broken neglect into two categories for easier identification.

- *Active Neglect*—the refusal or failure to fulfill a care-giving obligation, including conscious and intentional attempts to effect physical or emotional distress to the elder.
- *Passive Neglect*—the failure or refusal to fulfill a care-giving obligation with no aforethought or consideration of consequences. Passive neglect generally covers incompetent care-givers and self-neglect.[5]

Contrary to public perception, the majority of elder abuse takes place in their homes or apartments. Only 11 percent of all 85-year-olds and older move in with a grown child. The larger percentage of victims of abuse and neglect are women, primarily due to the fact that women outnumber men in the elder population.

It's not difficult to focus on neglect and abuse in the home when you realize that 'home' is still where most of the elderly live. Contrary to what you may have imagined, only 5 percent of persons 60 years and older live in institutions; only 8 percent of those 75-85 years of age are institutionalized, and, even though the numbers increase, still fewer than 25 percent of those 85 years of age and older reside in long-term care facilities.[6]

Since statistics show that the greater majority of elder persons live at home, it should not be too surprising (yet no less disturbing) to find that the source of abuse is more likely to be a family member. "Current research to be published by Karl Pillemer, Ph.D., indicates that the elderly are more likely to be abused by persons with whom they live—spouses, children, siblings, or other relatives."[7] There are four general factors in the cause of elder abuse and neglect.

- Physical and mental impairments of the victim—most notably contributing to self-neglect.
- External stresses on the abuser—such as the distressed care-giver.
- Learned behavior—such as the cycle of violence within a family.
- Individual problems of the abuser—such as a pathological abuser, irresponsible and age-fearing abusers.[8]

Drugs and alcohol are prevalent factors in the abuse of the elderly. Because alcohol and drugs diminish the inhibitions of an individual, they are more prone to abuse and neglect the elder family member. Counseling, and a greater understanding of the aging process and its accompanying problems, will go a long way in eliminating the problem of elder abuse and neglect.

One gerontologist takes up the issue of statistics on elder abuse. "Elder abuse is one of the fastest-growing crimes of our times, but it is mostly unreported and almost totally neglected in the budgets of local, state, and national government."[9] Therein lies the problem: There is very little reporting of elder abuse. However, the late Congressman Claude Pepper's House Subcommittee on Health and Long-Term Care held hearings on elder abuse in 1985. These are some of the shocking reports.

> A 75-year-old Massachusetts man, disguised in the hearings as "Mr. Smith," whose son had attacked him with a hatchet; a 74- year-old New Jersey woman whose son-in-law had beaten and raped her and whose daughter then threatened her, saying, "You won't have a home to sleep in if you say anything about this." Pepper's subcommittee estimated that, counting all forms, including unintentional neglect, "over 1,000,000 older Americans are physically, financially and emotionally abused by their relatives or loved ones annually." Surveys indicate that approximately *86 percent of the abused aged are victims of their own families.*[10] [italics mine]

Further statistics reveal that elder abuse is normally directed toward women who are 75+ years old and dependent on others to take care of them. Spouses are the most frequent perpetrators in elder abuse.[11] Because these elderly are most often frail, and thus incapable of defending themselves, they live in fear, saying nothing so as not to make things any worse. Douglas C. Kimmel reports that accurate data on the extent and nature of elder abuse are scarce.[12]

Is there a solution to this problem? Yes, I believe there is. More family members becoming involved in the care of aging parents will reduce or even eliminate abuses. Too often the care of a parent is left to one person. The rest of the family just seems to not want to be bothered.

THE DYSFUNCTIONAL FAMILY:
A CRISIS IN FAMILY COHESIVENESS

The term dysfunctional (abnormal or impaired in functioning[13]) is used in describing unhealthy families or attitudes exhibited by family members. In their book, *Family Therapy: An Overview*, Irene and Herbert Goldenberg address the importance of family therapy for the dysfunctional family.

> Family therapy locates conflict in the transactional interface between the individual and the dysfunctional family system. A disturbed person becomes trapped in a role designated for him or her by the family system, which results in impaired or arrested development. Efforts to become independent may lead to high levels of anxiety and guilt. Thus, the family context must be attended to in understanding the appearance of symptoms in a family member.[14]

Families today face different struggles than our forefathers did. Diseases that often wiped out whole communities are controlled, if not eliminated, by medication now. Financial pressures on families today exist because families either do not know how to budget, and therefore control their finances, or they feel the need to have more of an income to increase their purchasing power. In either event, the pressure is on! Families can't simply rely on eating what they grow since we are no longer primarily an agrarian society. Cash in the bank is needed to purchase the basics from those who provide these goods for us. Even if a person wanted to get back to an agrarian life style, it would nearly be impossible due to the enormous cost of land and its tillage. Having two brothers-in-law in farming, and a father-in-law who retired from farming, I have learned to sympathize with them in their desire to have a place of their own instead of working for someone else. Often I will encourage my two brothers-in-law to buy a place they could farm, but then they share with me the financial outlay required, despite the fact that they are both fiscally responsible, and it becomes apparent why such a venture is nearly impossible.

In bygone days the moral fiber of the country was strong and society adhered to its mores. Not so in the society of the 1990's. The traditional family values are routinely ridiculed in the media, television and even in our government. How can parents stand against such an onslaught? Many do not, and simply cave in to the morality of the moment, because tomorrow it will change from what it was today. "If a family is fragmented, divided into factions or unforgiving in its attitude toward its members, it will have painful times when trouble hits."[15] Trouble surely will hit, a fact of life for everyone. How the sandwich generation will handle caring for elderly parents is largely determined from the way they were raised. The more dysfunctional the family, the greater the chance of poor decisions being made on behalf of the elderly.

Pressures like these are brought to bear even on healthy families, families that are intact, and they struggle too. Families that are not healthy are virtually doomed from the outset.

One voice in the midst of our changing morality, speaking against the continued increase in dysfunctional families, is that of Billy Graham.

> A few years ago I had not heard the term "dysfunctional family" used as it is today. Now the concept is applied to so many that I begin to wonder how the family is functioning. In most parts of the world, it is not operating too well. I am not speaking only of the immediate family unit, but of the extended family and also the family of God. There is no need to review all the problems. You know them. In fact, you may be part of the problem. Only the strong Christian family unit can survive the increasing world crises.[16]

He presents a formula to counter the decline and potential demise of the traditional family unit. For those of the Christian faith it is straight forward.

> First, we need to place God at the center of our family. Second, as a family we need to walk with God daily. Third, consulting and memorizing Scripture as a family is vital. Together the family should read, mark, and learn the Scriptures as an essential preparation for the persecution ahead. Family prayer is a fourth vital link in the chain of spiritual strength—a strength we are trying to build to protect us from a world gone mad. Practicing prayer as a family, not just a flippant blessing before a meal, can give us the security we need.[17]

FEELINGS OF GUILT: A SHARED COMPLAINT

During the process of acquiring research information on the sandwich generation, it became apparent that those who were caring for their elderly parents, or were anticipating having to care for them, all shared one thing in common: guilt. This guilt manifested itself in two ways.

First, the elderly parent would make a comment to the adult child about how they wanted to be taken care of if they should lose the ability to care for themselves. The comment would go something like this. "Promise me you won't put me in one of those places. I don't ever want to be in there." "There," of course, is a nursing home, or any other place other than their own home and familiar surroundings that they are so accustomed to enjoying. The pressure placed on the adult child in being asked to make such a promise is heart-rending, to say the least.

Second, the adult child feels horrible when wrestling with the possibility of placing an elderly parent in "one of those places." I asked my dialogue group to share with me the most difficult part of being in the sandwich generation. As we moved around the circle, comment after comment confirmed that the single most challenging problem for them was dealing with guilt feelings. Each shared a similar scenario that had taken place with a parent where they had been asked, or made to promise, not to put the parent in a nursing facility. I was impressed with the amount of emotional turmoil that was expressed, accompanied by tears and frustration. Most felt it was not fair of the elderly parent to place them in such an impossible situation. Further discussion revealed a more practical approach to handling this guilt. Realizing the impossibility of caring for elderly parents at home indefinitely, many of the group had no qualms about placing their loved one in a nursing home. They could live with the guilt. Virtually to a person they agreed that the parent should be in their home as long as they were mentally competent. Once the mind was gone, as in the case of the onset of Alzheimer's disease (dementia), all agreed it was morally okay to admit the parent in a care facility where they could receive 24-hour attention. But the pain of such a decision was unmistakable. Knowing their actions to be the best ones for all concerned does not mean they are convinced that they are the right ones.

Jane Gould, 56, the director of aging, spent three years caring for her late mother, who suffered from Alzheimer's—rushing from her office in Albany to her mother's home in New York City. At work, she fielded phone calls. "I was talking to the doctor, the hospital, the social worker, the health aide and my mother," she recalled. "I'm still not sure I made all the right decisions. I feel guilty about not being there, about not giving enough time to my own family and my job."[18]

Guilt, whether self-induced or heaped upon the caregiver by the elderly parent(s), nags at the caregiver long after the loved one is gone. One of the ladies in my dialogue group has yet to reconcile her actions in providing care for her now-deceased mother. The fact that the rest of the group agreed that she had done all that was required and more, even acknowledging her actions to be justifiable, she could not shake the guilt.

NOTES

1. James Osterhaus, Family Ties Don't Have to Bind (Nashville: Thomas Nelson Publishers, 1994), 26-27.
2. James Dobson, Focus on the Family [Monthly newsletter], Nov. 1994, 3.
3. Buckler, 231.
4. Ibid., 232.
5. Ibid.
6. Ibid., 234.
7. Ibid., 235.
8. Ibid., 244.
9. Dychtwald, 243.
10. Ibid.
11. Kimmel, 505.
12. Ibid.
13. Goldenberg and Goldenberg, 328.
14. Ibid., 230.
15. Billy Graham, Hope for the Troubled Heart (Minneapolis: Grason, 1991), 175.
16. Ibid., 174.
17. Ibid., 174-75.
18. Winik, 5.

V
Multiple Generations:
Multiple Sandwiching

Statistically, it appears that the United States, in fact the whole world, is facing a new family condition that was once an oddity—namely, multiple generations living in the same time period. The question of who takes care of whom grows to immense proportions. Four, even five generational families are more the norm now than ever before in history. Having parents and their children both of retired age is occurring more and more frequently. There are a number of reasons for people living longer, thereby unintentionally and inadvertently creating this multi-generational condition. The biggest reason, and the most obvious, is the tremendous advancement in medical treatment, coupled with a nutritional diet and moderate exercise.

While maximum human survival may not have changed, unprecedented numbers of individuals are reaching their 9th, 10th, and 11th decades. Today there are 2.6 million Americans over age 85; when the post-World War II "baby boomers" reach this age, there will be 16 million. This group, the "oldest old," presents an important challenge to the field of geriatrics. Individuals in their sixties represent a relatively healthy group. It is in the late seventies and eighties when the diseases and disorders of aging take their profoundest toll. As a result, the chances of being in a chronic care institution increase exponentially in these later decades. In the U.S. approximately one in four over age 85 is in a nursing home.[1]

Kathie Erwin concludes her article, "Looking Backward, Looking Ahead—Helping Elders Cope," by stating that "in less than two decades, 20 percent of our population will be elders as the first wave of baby boomers start getting social security benefits. This aging trend is already felt among the older baby boomers who are facing the issues of caring for elder parents or dealing with friction in multi-generational households."[2]

There exists yet another aspect of the multiple generational issue. This occurs when adult offspring initially leave home, have children, and wind up returning to the family roost for what are a variety of reasons. Now the sandwich generation is caring for aging parents, grown children (at least biologically), and grandchildren. Conceivably, one generation could find itself taking care of aging grandparents, aging parents, adult children, and grandchildren.

In an article on the Internet entitled, "The Sandwich Generation: A Cluttered Nest," Herbert G. Lingren and Jayne Decker offer some valuable advice to those caught in the squeeze of caring for multiple generations. They say the middle years have been characterized as the "re-years." Words descriptive of this life phase begin with "re," a prefix meaning "to do again, to go back;" to reassess, reevaluate, rekindle, relearn, review, reappraise, restructure. To do this, people need to pursue the developmental tasks of mid-life. Developmental tasks are the skills, knowledge and attitudes needed at different points in their lives.

1. Launching children into responsible, happy adulthood.
2. Revitalizing their marriage.
3. Reviewing satisfaction and success concerning occupation or career.
4. Reorienting oneself to aging parents.
5. Realigning sex roles.
6. Reappraising where they are in terms of where they wanted to be by this time.[3]

Further, Lingren and Decker ask the following question: Can the challenges and complexities of multi-generational living be met? Listed below are several possible solutions for a meaningful and satisfying style of life:

1. Clarify the house rules.
2. Have a weekly family meeting.
3. Prepare a long-range financial plan.
4. Use available community programs and services.
5. Agree on a target date for departure for your young adult. Cut the apron strings.
6. Respect one another's privacy.
7. Take care of your own family, your marriage, and especially, take care of yourself.
   * Don't neglect your own family to take care of your parent.
   * Make caring for your parent a responsibility for the whole family.
   * Make everyone in the family aware of any problems.
   * If a parent moves into your home, that person should have their own room and phone.
   * Take the time for self-renewal.
   * Take time for your marriage.[4]

MEDICAL MILESTONES

What once were life-threatening illnesses are now treated oftentimes by over-the-counter drugs. What used to be literally the "kiss of death," may now be routinely treated in pristine hospitals, staffed by highly trained personnel. People expect to stay alive today. And not just stay alive, but to be made well again. Medical knowledge has multiplied at an amazing rate. Even that which is incurable today, such as AIDS and hepatitis B, is being researched with a vengeance. The general public believes that a cure will surely be found, and soon. After all, haven't we cured most every other disease and illness? We're on a roll, so to speak, and we expect this to continue.

The preamble of the Constitution of the World Health Organization states: 'The enjoyment of the highest attainable standard of health is one of the fundamental rights of every human being . . . .' Since 1946 when these words were written, the idea that health—or at least health care—is a matter of right has become so widely accepted as to be a commonplace.[5]

Along with the belief that Americans expect to be made well, there is the expectation that all medical facilities, and the far ranging possibilities of continued health, are virtually written into the Bill of Rights. Since so many of the deadly illnesses and diseases of the past have been controlled (at least in the United States, if not eradicated by modern-day medicine), life expectancy has now moved beyond being healed. With medical practice today, we enjoy a comfortable knowledge of personal health care that includes expensive equipment (such as CAT scans, or pace makers), medicine, specialized practitioners, artificial organs, blood for the treatment of hemophilia, donors for organ transplant operations, and research facilities.[6]

There is what is called the natural process of aging that takes place apart from medical intervention. This is a process that is an accepted function in life. In humans, there is a set of external manifestations or symptoms: greying [sic] hair, increased susceptibility to infection, wrinkling skin, loss of muscular tone, and frequently, loss of mental ability.[7] For the person who is facing the aging process, and the subtle changes and effects that aging brings to bear, there is a fear that life as it once was lived is no longer possible. And they are right. It is no longer possible to live and function as we once did. Perhaps a day will come when man is able to retard the aging process and lengthen his years, but that day is not yet here. The fear of losing control over the body and its natural functions, and the reduction in the performance of daily routine activities, has a depressing and debilitating effect on the aging person. Research has shown that depression is one of the most devastating effects of aging. Family plays a significant role here, offering love, support, and encouragement. With all the miracles attributed to modern science and medicine, family and human compassion are unequaled in the care of the elderly.

ALZHEIMER'S DISEASE: WHO IS THIS PERSON?

Virtually without argument, the most frightening prospect for the aging person is the thought that they will not have control over their thought processes. Many have expressed a foreboding and dread imagining a life where they are out of control, mentally. "At least if I have my mind," they muse, "I'll be okay." A prayer I have heard more than once goes like this: "Please God, don't let me lose my mind." "Cases of dementia and Alzheimer's in particular put an incredible strain on families," noted Dr. Rebecca Elon, medical director of the Johns Hopkins Geriatric Center in Baltimore.[8]

Alzheimer's (a form of dementia) has a grip of fear on many of our elderly today who approach their twilight years with apprehension. Sadly, many of our elderly are in the throes of Alzheimer's, out of touch with their world, their family and friends, and, worst of all, out of touch with themselves.

> [Alzheimer's] is the most devastating common geriatric disorder. It is manifested by gradually increasing confusion, disorientation, and loss of memory. The memory loss is severe, in contrast to the slight losses of recent memory that typically occur with normal aging.[9]

It is now projected that with the decrease in death by heart attack, strokes and heart disease, there will be an increase in the number of elderly who experience Alzheimer's. Some figures suggest there are one in three individuals in their eighties who have Alzheimer's, and that Alzheimer's disease will be the number one cause of death in the Twenty-first century.[10] Is it any wonder then that the elderly are fearful of this disease more than any other?

A recent article from Challenger magazine, entitled, "Alzheimer's Disease and Spirituality," identified Alzheimer's as the "disease of the century."[11] The description of the effects of the disease would cause anyone to reconsider the prospects of growing old. "It causes degeneration of the brain, manifested as a clinical dementia, causing impairment in memory and thinking, decline in language and motor capacity, with eventual loss of bodily functions and total inability to care for oneself."[12] In a word: a nightmare! In the *DSM-III-R*, under "Organic Mental Syndromes and Disorders," a description is given of this dementia, listing three levels of criteria for severity.

- *Mild*: Although work or social activities are significantly impaired, the capacity for independent living remains, with adequate personal hygiene and relatively intact judgment.
- *Moderate*: Independent living is hazardous, and some degree of supervision is necessary.
- *Severe*: Activities of daily living are so impaired that continual supervision is required, e.g., unable to maintain minimal personal hygiene; largely incoherent or mute.[13]

In a recent issue of *U.S. News & World Report* magazine there is a brief article about progress being made in the fight against Alzheimer's. According to the article researchers have been able to create a strain of mouse that suffers from this disease.

"It's a fantastic mouse," said John Trojanowski, director of the University of Pennsylvania Alzheimer's Center. "This has the potential to change the field overnight." To create the new strain, scientists at Athena Neuroscience's, a company in South San Francisco, dosed mice with one of the genes for human Alzheimer's. The resulting animals have many of the brain symptoms seen in humans with Alzheimer's. Athena now plans to test whether the mice also suffer memory loss.[14]

There are those who help us deal with the effects of aging in a humorous vein. One such person is Bill Cosby. In his book, *Time Flies*, he recounts his growing awareness that he is forgetting things more frequently, and that his mind is playing tricks on him. Though what follows is not a medical case of identifiable Alzheimer's, it is the sort of predicament a person experiences in the aging process that causes them to wonder if they are in the early stages of the disease. We'll pick up his story of heading to work with his attaché case.

One more time, you pick up the shirts, the attaché case, and then softly say to whatever puckish powers run the universe, "Now what the hell did I do with the insect spray?"

You're losing it, old boy, says your mind.

"You mean the insect spray?" you reply.

No, much more than that.

"Nonsense; I'm just tired."

Really? Then where is the spray?

"In the attaché case."

Okay, look, says your mind.
"I don't *have* to look; I know it's there," you reply, continuing to talk to yourself without moving your lips.
You're afraid to look.
"No, I'm not."
And you open the case, try not to look inside, and you find the spray nestled mockingly there. You now decide to stop thinking about what you are carrying and go to work at once, hoping that you will not arrive at the office in your Jockey shorts.
Wait a minute. . . . Did you remember to put them on?
And did you also remember that when you were young, you never dreamed that anything like this could happen to you? A young man has absolutely no notion that life will one day turn him into one of the Three Stooges. . . . But now I know only too well that the mind of a man my age is a magician who could play Radio City.[15] [italics in original]

Equally as humorous is a chapter entitled "The Race Against Time" in Andy Rooney's book, *Not That You Asked* . . .

Well, it looks now as though it's going to be a race against time for those of us past forty years old to see whether we live forever. They keep chipping away at the things that are killing people and it looks as though there's a good chance they'll have everything licked in our lifetime. . . . The scientific and medical communities are going to have to step up the speed of their inventions, preventions and discoveries if they hope to have all the illnesses known to the human mind and body either cured or preventable before one of them catches up with us. Some of us don't have all the time in the world left. What I want, if any of you medical scientists are reading this, is a small pill that can be taken once a day before dinner, with a martini, that will cure anything I already have and prevent anything I might catch in the future. In addition to inhibiting cancer, heart disease, cirrhosis of the liver, kidney failure and shingles, I'd expect this little pill to keep me from getting Alzheimer's and palsy and at the same time restore any names to my memory that I can't think of. Neither do I want to read a lot of warnings on the label telling me that if I take too much of the stuff it could produce bad side effects. This all-purpose, live-forever pill should be 100 percent side-effects-less. I know you medical scientists can do it if you put your minds to it. If some of you were a

little older, you might have more incentive to work harder on the
problem. . . . Just as soon as science has licked old age and all the
diseases we humans die of, we're going to have to face the problem of
where all of us are going to live. If no one ever dies, there's going to
be a honey of a housing shortage. . . . this is going to be one crowded
planet in another hundred years.[16]

"The onset of Alzheimer's disease is often subtle and may pass
unnoticed except in retrospect," says Florence Lau in her article on
Alzheimer's disease and spirituality.

Forgetfulness and behavioral changes are often mistakenly attributed
to "normal" aging. While it is true that all of us will occasionally forget
a person's name or misplace the car keys as we get older, the
distinguishing characteristic of the memory lapses in the Alzheimer's
patient is that he will not know who the person is whose name he has
forgotten, and he will not remember how to use the car keys even if he
were to find them. These changes in the Alzheimer's disease patient
are permanent and progressive. Recent memory is lost first, while
remote memories such as those from childhood remain intact longer.[17]

The impact of Alzheimer's on family members is devastating. Who
is this person that they have known and loved for so many years? Where
have they gone? Here is where the sandwich generation often finds itself
stumped as to what to do. During my dialogue sessions with my sandwich generation group, I kept hearing people say that their loved ones
would beg them never to put them into "one of those places." More often
was the effort on the elderly person to get their adult child to promise
them they would not have them committed to a nursing home or some
other institution. The agony expressed by the members in my dialogue
group as to what to do was heart-rending. This part of the groups
interaction most frequently brought out the need for a tissue box.
      The general consensus of the group was that when an elderly parent
or loved one no longer had their mental faculties working for them (as in
Alzheimer's) then having them admitted to a nursing home where they
could receive round-the-clock care was acceptable, and highly preferable.
In my own situation with my ninety-three-year-old grandmother,

Bambin, admitting her to a nursing home was the most difficult decision I have ever had to make, bar none.

> When the diagnosis of Alzheimer's disease is made, the patient and family react with profound grief. The various stages of grieving may be encountered from denial to depression to final resignation or acceptance. What makes Alzheimer's disease particularly hard is that in addition to the physical deterioration, there is also erosion of mental faculties and the disintegration of the individual's unique personality. The very coping mechanisms for dealing with serious illnesses, are unavailable to the Alzheimer's patient as the disease advances.[18]

While a seminary student I was doing some radio work with a missionary, himself quite elderly. He and his wife had spent many years on the mission field, but due to advancing age they retired back in the States. His wife's mother was living with them and had developed a severe case of Alzheimer's. The couple was committed to her and rarely left the home together. They told me that she used to be a "spiritual giant," "a woman of prayer." However, some of the things I heard coming out of her mouth from upstairs gave pause for consideration. The foulest language, the kind I was accustomed to during my Marine Corps days, would come out of this dear old saint's mouth. Not only was it embarrassing for this couple, it left them stupefied and helpless as to what to do. Curiously though, if you asked the woman to pray, she would launch into the sweetest phrases of praise and adoration heard this side of heaven. Not one word would there be to make a person blush or consider anything to be wrong. This alone gave the missionary couple hope and comfort for their loved one.

One pastor, Reverend Robert Davis, wrote about his own experience of entering into the horror of Alzheimer's in his book, *My Journey into Alzheimer's Disease*. "Fear and doubt about [one's] spiritual standing with God are common," he writes. "The victim's predicament is incomprehensible and he may feel angry and even betrayed by God."[19]

Florence Lau offers several suggestions as to what others can do to help. She recommends two books that deal specifically with Alzheimer's. *The 36-Hour Day*, by Nancy L. Mace and Peter V. Rabins, and

Alzheimer's: Caring for Your Loved One; Caring for Yourself, are both very practical.

> As the disease advances, the Alzheimer's patient is less able to cope with new situations. Thus it is important that his surroundings and daily schedule be as familiar and routine as possible. As short-term memory declines, reminders from the distant past such as stories, experiences, and pictures can help anchor him to reality. Even though the patient regresses, it is still important to treat him with respect.
>
> Currently there is no cure for Alzheimer's disease. A palliative treatment (Tacrine) may arrest the progression of the disease for about six months, but it is expensive and a number of patients experience significant side effects.[20]

Further, she makes several suggestions regarding the spiritual welfare of the Alzheimer's patient.

> For as long as it is physically possible, the believer with Alzheimer's disease should be encouraged to attend worship services. The familiar liturgy, hymns and prayers can be a source of spiritual reassurance. Local church members can be a vital link to the spiritual well-being of the patient and his family who undergo tremendous stresses during the course of the illness. When reading is impossible for the patient, other believers can tape Bible readings or favorite hymns for him to listen to. Bible passages that tell of God's promises are especially comforting. Praying for the individual is always welcome, but practical assistance in the form of running errands, helping with household chores, preparing a meal, or providing a respite for the tired caregiver can show others the love of Christ through us.[21]

Many elderly people see their later years as a cruel joke compared to what they once were. O! To have vim and vigor again! To not be a burden on anyone. To just quietly leave this life behind. But it is not always so. Chuck Swindoll, well-known pastor, radio preacher, and author, offers these words of encouragement to those in their twilight years in his book, *Growing Strong in the Seasons of Life*, under the chapter entitled, "Growing Old."

No one fails to see that growing old has its difficulties and heartaches. It does, indeed. But to see only the hot sands of your desert experience and miss the lovely oases here and there (though they may be few) is to turn the latter part of your journey through life into an arid, tasteless endurance which makes everyone miserable.

Please don't forget—God has decided to let you live this long. Your old age is not a mistake. . . . nor an oversight. . . . nor an afterthought. Isn't it about time you cooled your tongue and softened your smile with a refreshing drink from the water of God's oasis? You've been thirsty a long, long time."[22]

The family that is facing the prospect of living with a loved one who is in the grip of Alzheimer's disease will do well to consider the words of encouragement given by Chuck Swindoll.

Ironically, former president Ronald Reagan has been diagnosed with Alzheimer's disease. In a letter to the American people in November of 1995, Reagan wrote of his descent into Alzheimer's. It had been coming on for the last two to three years. Friends have recently visited with Reagan and said his condition has grown significantly worse. This dreaded disease is no respecter of persons.

During an interview on my radio program, *Solutions for Life*, with talk show host, Michael Reagan, he shared some insight he had gained from his father's bout with Alzheimer's.

You have to remember the good times. You have to remember the wonderful times together. It's easier to converse with them if you converse at the level they're at. If I go in and visit my dad and my dad wants to talk about the `30s when he was a life guard, then be a life guard with him. Be on the banks of the river in Illinois where he saved seventy-seven lives. And listen to him tell you the story. It doesn't matter that you've heard it for three hundred times. It's the first time to him again. So what I do is listen. Where dad is, I'll be at. And I have great conversations with him. They're not long conversations. But I have great short conversations with him. I talk to him wherever his level is at. And the last thing I want to do, and I don't ever do, is change the subject.[23]

In the biomedical report of *Christian Counseling Today* magazine, Roger Sider states in his article that there are five warning signs of possible impaired brain function in the age group over 50. They are:

- Periods of confusion or disorientation—even if temporary.
- A decline in appearance and grooming—particularly if there does not seem to be awareness of this neglect.
- Short-term memory loss—difficulty remembering what one ate at the last meal or where one went yesterday.
- Impaired judgement—unwise decisions with regard to money or relationships.
- A change of personality—the client no longer seems like himself.[24]

Unless a cure is discovered for Alzheimer's, the disease will only continue to claim more victims, according to the statistical data of the Alzheimer's Association. In 1990 there were an estimated 3.8 million Americans affected by Alzheimer's. In just fifty-five years, A.D. 2050, that number is projected to be 10.2 million.[25]

THE RIGHT TO DIE (EUTHANASIA)

The advances of medical science have contributed enormously to the socially volatile issue of a person's having the right to choose how they want to die. This is not a new topic in the history of the world, but certain aspects of the issue are new. As mentioned, with the technological advances that now prolong life, does anyone, particularly those in the medical profession, have the right to assist someone in terminating their life? Clearly, this issue today has as much of a polarizing effect as the abortion issue has had and continues to have. It shows no indications of being resolved any time soon. In fact, the recent elections in Oregon have produced a further twist in the right to die quagmire.

Oregon passed a ballot measure allowing doctors to prescribe lethal doses of drugs with the patient's consent. Granted, there are a number of restrictions in this measure (Measure 16), but many would say that Pandora's box has been opened.

The new Oregon law will leave it up to individual doctors, whose professional oath requires them to do nothing that would cause a patient harm, to decide whether or not to comply with someone's request to die. The request must be in writing, and the patient must be judged to have less than six months to live—the legal definition for terminally ill under the act. The law also exempts doctors from civil or criminal or criminal liability if they have acted in "good faith compliance" with the law.[26]

This current event seems to fly in the face of the professional code long held by the medical profession. Historically, doctors have been required to swear to the creeds of the Hippocratic Oath in which they state, "I will neither give a deadly drug to anybody if asked for it, nor will I make a suggestion to this effect. . . . In purity and holiness I will guard my life and my art."[27]

From the Oath it is clear that a doctor has sworn not to give any person a drug overdose in an attempt to end their life. Even more revealing is the remark that the doctor will not even make the suggestion. Two arguments can be put forth in determining some course of action for the medical professional. First, the Hippocratic Oath could be regarded as antiquated and out of touch, especially in light of the tremendous advances in medicine. Hippocrates, the father of medicine, lived approximately 400 years before Christ. A lot has changed since then. Additionally, the Oath did not actually come into existence until 1747. Second, the development of vaccinations and life-prolonging medicines, coupled with unimaginable technological advancements, necessitates a closer examination of the requirements of the medical profession.

There are arguments countering a person's right to die, even if assisted by a physician. First, the determination as to the value of human life must be considered. Does any one person have the right to end a life, even if it is their own? Second, there is the valid concern expressed in allowing a person, or a body of people, to adjudge a person's fitness to live. Where is the line drawn? Third, the elderly often assert their feelings about being hospitalized and then find themselves in the hands of a doctor who does not regard their life as worth the effort to save. Granted, the patient is to be consulted. But if the patient is in a critical condition and cannot speak for themselves, what's to keep the doctor from deciding for the patient before anything else can be done? Who would know?

The ethical decisions and their ramifications are staggering. Tom Beauchamp states, "The killing/allowing to die debate includes two distinct subquestions: Is it possible to draw a clear, logical distinction between actions and omissions? And, if such an action can be drawn, is it morally relevant?"[28] It is not the purpose of this book to resolve this issue. However, it is an issue that sandwiched families must consider. They more than likely will be making decisions for loved ones, forcing them to address these questions. An adult child could face the possibility of an elderly parent being "incompetent" in making decisions in certain matters.[29] This is a prospect no adult child wants to contemplate.

The Oregon measure (assisted-suicide law) has caused debate and concern in the medical community. Mark Skinner, a general internist in Portland, is troubled by Measure 16. "It bothers me. I don't know how to deal with it. I can conceive of myself being in a position to make such a decision, but I honestly don't know what I would do."[30] The article went on to say that the Oregon medical community is divided over the issue of physician assisted-suicide. The American Medical Association, on the other hand, has come out in opposition to the measure. Such conditions merely compound the dilemma faced by family members who must attempt to make such crucial decisions for loved ones.

SINGLE-PARENT FAMILIES

There exists today a growing problem in society in regard to the role of the care-giver due to the increasing number of single-parent families. It is readily apparent that a single-parent (or single adult child) is going to find it much more challenging to take care of an elderly parent(s) without the support both financially and emotionally of a spouse. Since it traditionally falls to the woman to provide such care, she may find herself in the unenviable position of working at a lower paying job, longer-hours, therefore less time and money to assist in caring for an elderly parent(s).

Recent statistics indicate the alarming rise in single-parent families in the United States. A graph put out by the U.S. Bureau of the Census shows that in 1960 only 9.1 percent of all families with children were single-parent families. That figure has tripled (28.6 percent) in the last three decades.

Today, 17 million children live in single-parent homes. According to the U.S. Bureau of the Census, 55 percent of children in Detroit live in single-parent homes, 53 percent in Washington, D.C., and 49 percent in Atlanta. Approximately 90 percent of single-parent homes are homes without a father.[31]

Of those in my dialogue group who are single-parents, they share a common frustration: There's not enough of them, or their funds, to go around. If the elderly parent needs care, it means Susie doesn't get her braces now, if ever. It could mean canned beans and bread for supper for a while. Or it could mean the elderly parent isn't given the needed care. The single-parent must establish priorities concerning spending on both children and parent.

The single-parent/adult child faces yet another dilemma in the struggle to be a proper care-giver. Certain problems are endemic to being a single-parent. William Galston writes in "A Progressive Family Policy for the 1990's," in Mandate for Change that the problems faced by the single-parent are disturbing, to say the least.

The economic consequences of a parent's absence are often accompanied by psychological consequences, which include higher than average levels of youth suicide, low intellectual and educational performance, and higher than average rates of mental illness, violence and drug use.[32]

It is most disturbing to see the teen suicide rate rising so rapidly. This seems to support the statement just cited indicating "higher than average levels of youth suicide." Because of these statistics and others, many of the single-parents that I know are fearful of the direction their child(ren) is taking in life. In an effort to provide a special ministry to single-parents, I sought to develop a group ministry in the church I most recently was serving in. Before going too far I was advised by several living in this single-parent predicament that they were not interested nearly so much in being with other single-parents as much as to be around families that at least appeared to be healthy (i.e., mother/father/kids). Thus, the single-parent joins Sunday school classes and Bible study groups where there is a positive mix of families. In particular, they want their children to have the exposure to a family where there is an active mother, father and children, preferably children of the same age. Many of the single mothers hope some man in the congregation will take an active interest in their son if for no other reason than to be a role-model. The church I previously served in has a ministry in this area, linking young boys to men as a means of helping these young boys develop into godly men (Titus 2:6-8).

THE BOTTOM LINE: THE FAMILY MATTERS

Considering every aspect of caring for elderly parents by the family, it is the family unit, individual by individual, that is going to be there to provide the love, care, compassion and encouragement for those who are in the final years of their life. We have considered the change in our family structure in the last number of decades through the advances of medical science. The government will undoubtedly continue to play a role in the care of the elderly (Chapter 3). Churches will be pressed to be more involved in elder care, becoming more creative in that area of ministry (see Chapter 6). Families would profit by becoming knowledgeable concerning all the avenues available to them in the care of their elderly parents, taking advantage of each one that is appropriate.

Parents who have loved and cared for their own children through the years can expect the same level of care, love, and respect reciprocated when they are faced with the uncertainties of the aging process. It will be the children who will stand by their aging parents faithfully, seeing to their care, knowing that no one else would ever be able to care for the loved one the way they do.

The importance of family relationships cannot be overstated. We often limit our thinking in this area to the present. Yet one of the most cherished possessions I have are the memoirs of my great-grandfather,

Reverend Daniel Thatcher Lake. In his own words he explains his reluctance to record his life's story.

> I have been solicited time and again to write up a sketch of my life and labors, but I have felt that I have done so little in the Master's Vineyard, and therefore so unworthy, that I have hesitated long about saying anything of myself. But as I am now past my three score years, and fast going down the hillside of life, if ever I leave anything on record for the satisfaction of my family and friends, it must be done soon, or not at all. Therefore I send this imperfect sketch, hoping it may result in good, especially to the young men of our church.[42]

What a priceless document these memoirs are to me and my family! He describes his childhood growing up in a boarding house run by his stepfather; how he attended school a few weeks each summer in an attempt to educate himself; how he became a teacher; then a preacher of the gospel; served in the Confederate Army, was wounded, and became known as the "Fighting Parson." He ministered as a circuit-riding preacher for more than three decades. What a treasure would have been lost had he not been prevailed upon to record his life's work.

For the past several years I have been encouraging my mother, now in her ninth decade, to record her life's story. She is presently working on it and will produce an excellent accounting of her personal history. I want my children's children to enjoy reading a record of their great-grandmother which can then be passed to succeeding generations.

Bobb Biehl, in his book, *Weathering the Midlife Storm*, has a section entitled, Memories: Relating As an Adult to Future Generations of the Family.

> One of the great tragedies is the fact that we die before we are able to relate to our great-great-great-grandchildren - adult to adult. One of my deep regrets was the fact that I knew all four of my grandparents until I was in my late teens and early twenties but did not have the maturity to seek an adult conversation with them about what their lives were like at my age.
>
> One of the things you might want to consider at this point in your life is filling out a memories book. A memories book is simply a guided diary. It tells what your life as an adult has been in the past,

what it's like currently, what you hope it will be someday. You write down what you see as an adult, about how you see life, what your experience with God has been, what your experience with people has been, what your experience with your parents has been. It basically helps you write your personal and family history.

There will come a day when your children or grandchildren will want to know what you (dad or mom, aunt or uncle, grandfather or grandma), were like as an adult. What were you thinking? What were your struggles?

It is a way to communicate adult-to-adult with future generations about your experience with God, your struggles, how you came to faith, and actually share your faith with your grandchildren and great-great-great-great-great-grandchildren, ten generations from now. It's an unusual way to look at it, but it's adult-to-adult conversation/relationship between you and all future generations of your family. Consider it as a possibility.[34]

NOTES

1. Edward L. Schneider, "Aging," in *1987 Medical and Health Annual* (Chicago: Encyclopedia Britannica, 1987), 270.

2. Erwin, 36.

3. "The Sandwich Generation: A Cluttered Nest," Herbert G. Lingren and Jayne Decker, in *NebGuide*, http://ianrwww.unl.edu/ianr/PUBS/extnpubs/family/g11 17.htm #expectations; 1996.

4. Ibid.

5. Joseph M. Boyle, Jr., "The Concept of Health and the Right to Health Care," in *On Moral Medicine*, eds. Stephen E. Lammers and Allen Verhey (Grand Rapids: Eerdmans Publishing, 1987), 643.

6. Robert Nozick, "The Allocation of Medical Resources," in *Contemporary Issues in Bioethics*, eds. Tom L. Beauchamp and LeRoy Walters, 3rd ed. (Belmont, Calif.: Wadsworth Publishing, 1989). 553.

7. Arthur L. Caplan, "The 'Unnaturalness' of Aging: A Sickness unto Death?" in *Contemporary Issues in Bioethics*, eds. Tom L. Beauchamp and LeRoy Walters, 3rd ed. (Belmont, Calif.: Wadsworth Publishing, 1989), 107.

8. Winik, 6.

9. Schneider, 271.

10. Ibid.

11. Florence Lau, "Alzheimer's Disease and Spirituality," *Challenger*, Oct. 1994, 1.

12. Ibid.

13. *Diagnostic Criteria from DSM-III-R*, ed. Janet B. W. Williams (Washington, D.C.: American Psychiatric Association, 1987), 80.

14. "New Troopers in the Alzheimer's War: Mice," *U.S. News & World Report*, 20 Feb. 1995, 18.

15. Bill Cosby, *Time Flies* (New York: Bantam Books, 1987), 58-59.

16. Andrew A. Rooney, *Not That You Asked* . . . (New York: Penguin Books, 1990), 22-23.

17. Lau, 2.

18. Ibid.

19. Robert Davis, *My Journey Into Alzheimer's Disease* (Wheaton, IL.: Tyndale House, 1989), 33.

20. Lau, 2.

21. Ibid.

22. Charles R. Swindoll, *Growing Strong in the Seasons of Life* (Portland: Multnomah Press, 1983), 349.

23. Michael Reagan, *Solutions for Life*, KCBC Radio Transcript, Oakdale, Calif., 13 January 1997.

24. Roger Sider, "The Brain Goes through Stages Too," *Christian Counseling Today*, (July 1993), 37.

25. "New Troopers," 18.

26. Timothy Egan, "Assisted-Suicide Law Will Put Oregon on Uncharted Path," *Fresno* [Calif.] *Bee*, 25 Nov. 1994, A14.

27. Oswei Temkin and C. Lillian Temkin, "Hippocratic Oath," in *Contemporary Issues in Bioethics*, eds. Tom L. Beauchamp and LeRoy Walters, 3rd ed. (Belmont, Calif.: Wadsworth Publishing, 1989), 310.

28. William H. Harris and Judith S. Levey, "Euthanasia and the Prolongation of Life," in *Contemporary Issues in Bioethics*, eds. Tom L. Beauchamp and LeRoy Walters, 3rd ed. (Belmont, Calif.: Wadsworth Publishing, 1989), 240.

29. Ibid., 242.

30. Egan.

31. William J. Bennett, *The Index of Leading Cultural Indicators*, vol. 1 (Washington, D.C.: The Heritage Foundation/Empower America, 1993), 16.

32. William Galston and Elaine Kamarck, "A Progressive Family Policy for the 1990's," in *The Index of Leading Cultural Indicators*, ed. William J. Bennett, vol. 1 (Washington, D.C.: The Heritage Foundation/Empower America, 1993), 16.

33. Rev. Daniel Thatcher Lake, *The Life and Times of Reverend Daniel Thatcher Lake, 1828-1891* personal memoirs written between 1889-91.

34. Bobb Biehl, *Weathering the Midlife Storm* (Victor Books, 1996), 154-155.

VI
The Role of the Church:
A Viable Ministry?

THE CHURCH MUST FILL THE GAP

The sandwich generation will apparently continue to play a major role in the care of the elderly. So then, what part does the church play in assisting both the elderly and the families? With society relegating the elderly to a non-useful role, the church has an excellent opportunity to take full advantage of their time and talents. One pastor writes of a pastorate he served and how the backbone of the church's ministry was a group of elderly persons who lived in apartments in the neighborhood.

> Persons like Mary Boyce and Quincy Potter, who, in their late 80's, with very little financial resources of their own, would spend long hours visiting with neighborhood families, letting them know that they were loved, that they were important. What these wonderful ladies had to give was themselves. They would spend hours listening, caring, sharing themselves and their faith. The richness of these ladies was not measured in doing or having, but in being. They were what they were. Nothing was hidden. There was no attempt to be something else. There was no excuse for poverty or lacking anything. They were delightfully genuine, honest, open, real. All the barriers were torn down. This is the vulnerability and the blessing of the elderly. It is their gift to us.[1]

Within certain ethnic groups and societies, the elderly are revered and respected at times over other age groups. By the fact that the elderly have lived as long as they have affords them a right to some respect.

Within certain religious communities, this gift, or blessing of the elderly, the mature, is given a place of honor.

> In Judaism aged persons and scholars should be treated with special respect. The rabbis apply the verse: 'Thou shalt rise up before the hoary head, and honor the face of the old man' (Leviticus 19:23) to scholars as well as to the aged, and rule that one should rise to one's feet as a token of respect whenever an old man or a scholar passes by (Kiddushin 32b). Some of the rabbis would show respect even to aged pagans because, they argued, they have been through so much in their long lives (Kiddushin 33a).[2]

TEACH THE CHURCH TO HONOR THE ELDERLY

Reverend Robert Alexander expresses strong views of the importance of the church to honor and respect the elderly.

> I find that there is a relationship between the place of honor or respect given to the elderly within a religious community and the desire of the community to live out a religious tradition. If a religious community, church or synagogue pays little attention to its traditions, its roots, it will not provide a place of honor for its elderly.[3]

In a recent newsletter from David L. Rambo, president of the Christian and Missionary Alliance denomination, he expressed what he saw as the greatest challenges facing churches. The first challenge he listed was for churches to "develop an enlightened ministry to seniors, the fastest-growing segment of society."[4]

The contribution that the elderly can make in the life of the religious community cannot afford to be overlooked. At my mother's former church in Fresno, California, Saint Luke's United Methodist, they have a group for the elderly called the "Triple L Club." This group of elderly congregants meets monthly for times of sharing and encouragement, as well as seeking to be involved some way in the community. The triple L means *Living Long and Loving it*. In another church where I served on the pastoral staff, the minister for the seniors had his hands full, what with all the outings these folks went on and the ministry opportunities that were created. This group called themselves the "X, Y, Z'ers." In addition, the elderly often have vast amounts of training and expertise that could be well used in the church, experience that they would love to use to the good of everyone.

Involvement in the life of the religious community can be a very invigorating experience for the elderly, as noted in the story of Mary and Quincy mentioned earlier. This can be a source of renewed hope in life for the elderly person, feeling that they are needed and have something to contribute. It also gives them something to look forward to on a regular basis.

For the sandwich generation (the extended family of the elderly), the church becomes a place of counsel, support and encouragement. Having an elderly parent to care for is strenuous work both physically and emotionally, and possibly financially. The church may well be a source of help in all three of these areas. The pastor and staff should be seen as a support team to the family, and the congregation should be seen as a well of resources to be available as needed.

The elderly may find that they are no longer able to make what some might consider significant contributions to the life of the church. In response to that, one elderly woman put it like this:

> Reverend, I am nearly 90 years of age. I do not see very well anymore, and I cannot hear much. Many people wonder why I even bother to come to church, because I cannot sing the songs, and I can barely hear the message. I guess I come because I just want people to know that I still love God, and I still believe God loves me. I just want people to know, after 88 years, whose side I'm on.[5]

For many elderly, one reason for church attendance is to be involved in the community and to take part in the social life of the church. In 1985, a Gallup Public Opinion Poll "indicated that the average weekly attendance at church or synagogue of persons over 65 years of age is 49 percent. This is 7 percentage points above the average for adults of all ages who attend weekly services at a church or synagogue."[6] People attend church for a variety of reasons, but recent studies show why the

elderly are so committed to the church, and in making their presence
known.

> During the senior years, church attendance is related to a deepening of
> personal faith and the reassurance of immortality. There are
> contradictions to these general findings, but the point I wish to draw is
> that, as a person matures, his or her faith commitment has little to do
> with pleasing others or keeping status within the community and much
> to do with a deeper personal commitment to God and to the assurance
> of life after death.[7]

The church needs to take an activist role in its ministry to, and
involvement with, seniors. The focus must be on others and not on self.
Nor do the elderly just want to sit around and do nothing. Maggie Kuhn,
one of the founders of the Gray Panthers Movement, expresses concern
that the church has been influenced by the values of society, especially in
its treatment of the elderly. Commenting on "Golden Age Clubs," she
says, "They trivialize old age, assuming that all people want to do in their
old age is play—just one round of merriment after another. Many of my
peers are conditioned to believe that they deserve to play after years of
hard work."[8] She goes on to ask a hard question.

> How does this prepare anyone to deal with the anger that is within us
> all growing old? The sheer terror of not having enough money, of
> acquiring some crippling disease, cannot be dispensed with fun and
> games. One old man said to me, with some disgust: "My God, I've
> made ashtrays for everybody I know. Can I give you an ashtray?" This
> is not to downgrade play, but play on these terms is such a waste. . . .
> It's a waste of experience, of years of being able to cope. Play does not
> help us to develop positive new images of strength. Some churches are
> providing services: Meals on Wheels, friendly visiting, transportation,
> etc. Services are fine; they are needed, but they won't change the
> prevailing value system.[9]

Not to be overlooked, the church secretary plays a significant part in
the ministry to the elderly. This caregiver faces the enormous responsibility of often having to make arrangements for pastoral hospital calls,
setting up the necessary details of a funeral (since the family may not be

emotionally capable), and notifying family in the event that no family members are in the immediate area at the time of death. It was estimated that in 1994 there would be "an estimated two million funerals in the United States."[10]

The opportunity for the church to take a role of responsibility with the elderly is both activistic and futuristic. People want to be involved in life. They want to be active, if at all possible. The church has a responsibility to meet this need for the senior citizen. This, too, is ministry. But, then there is the need to look to the future. The church must recognize that people are living longer, and therefore the breadth of ministry to the elderly must increase to meet the need, or the church will lose a precious and valuable support system.

A tongue-in-cheek view of old age was written by Virgene Clark, revealing societies views and attitudes toward the elderly. Those who are 80+ know exactly what she is saying, and those of us who are not at that age in life would do well to give it serious contemplation.

LIFE BEGINS AT 80

I have good news for you. The first 80 years are the hardest. The second 80 are a succession of birthday parties.

Once you reach 80, everyone wants to carry your baggage and help you up the steps. If you forget your name or anybody else's name, or an appointment, or your own telephone number, or promise to be three places at one time, or can't remember how many grandchildren you have, you need only to explain that you are 80.

Being 80 is a lot better than being 70. At 70, people are mad at you for everything. At 80, you have a perfect excuse no matter what you do. If you act foolishly, it's your second childhood. Everybody is looking for symptoms of softening of the brain.

Being 70 is no fun at all. At that age they expect you to retire to a house in Florida and complain about your arthritis (they used to call it lumbago) and you ask everyone to stop mumbling because you cannot understand them. (Actually, your hearing is about 50 percent gone.)

If you survive until you are 80, everybody is surprised that you are still alive. They treat you with respect just for having lived so long. Actually, they are surprised that you can walk and talk sensibly.

So please, folks, try to make it to 80. It's the best time of life. People forgive you for anything. If you ask me, life begins at 80.[11]

Finally, there is an interesting section of scripture in 1 Tim. 5:1-2. It bears thoughtful consideration.

Do not rebuke an older man harshly, but exhort him *as if he were your father.* Treat younger men as brothers, *older women as mothers* [italics mine], and younger women as sisters, with absolute purity.

This teaching is a must for the church if it ever hopes to recapture the proper perspective it is to have toward the elderly. When respect is given up and down the line between generations, a harmony of spirit is evident. Even if a person has had poor role models as mothers and fathers, respectfulness is always appropriate and honors God. Therein lies the beauty of the Golden Rule: Do to others as you would have them do to you (Luke 6:31). So it should be in the church and between generations.

CONCERNS OF THE AGING

As the church takes seriously the role of support in caring for its aging members, one article in particular addresses the concerns shared by many of our elderly as they move further into their later years. Eleanor McKinney, a seventy-four-year-old great-grandmother of four, works tirelessly alongside her pastor husband at Valley Hope Community Church in Turlock, California. She is an author and international speaker and has lived the concerns she writes about in an article she wrote for *Just Between Us.*

The younger generation looks to older, mature Christians for guidance and encouragement, but who sits down with the "Sixty-Something" and asks them, "How are things going in your life? Is there anything you would care to talk about? How can I pray for you? Is there some specific need that I could help with?" It may be surprising to learn that, yes, they are hurting, they are worried, they are filled with anxiety.[12]

She goes on to say that it is most important to listen to the conversations of the elderly. What do they talk about the most? Health problems! This is their biggest concern. This is where you begin to minister to them by demonstrating an understanding attitude as you begin to deal with their unique needs and concerns.

THE FIVE COMMON CONCERNS OF THIS AGE GROUP

1. *Failing health*: Those trips to the doctor may be coming more often. Their aches and pains seem endless. They try to keep up the pace they were going ten years ago but find they're running out of steam too early. Days are spent waiting for the medical test results, though they pretend not to be worried and say they are just routine.

2. *Financial concerns*: Many people think they had saved enough for that rainy day, only to find their resources have eroded, due to the rising cost of living or other unexpected reasons that have eaten away at their savings. They worry, "Will I have enough funds to take care of me for the rest of my life?" and "What about Social (In)Security?"

3. *Death/Widowhood*: If both spouses are living, the big question facing them is, "Which one of us will pass away first?" "If I die before my spouse, how will he/she make it alone?" "If my spouse dies first, what will I do? Can I make it by myself?" No one wants to become a burden to their children. Thoughts that go through their minds may be, "How will I die?" "Will it be long and painful?" "Will my insurance be sufficient to cover rising funeral costs?"

4. *Physical aging*: This may be easily accepted by some, but others are reminded every time they look in the mirror that aging is not a friend. They remember times without wrinkles, graying hair, "crows feet" in the corner of their eyes, obesity and sagging muscles. Their own reflection talks back to them and they don't like what they hear or see. They know it is a losing battle between

their desires and Mother Nature. Be patient and understanding with those who continue to try looking young and give them lots of praise. No one ever tires of hearing someone say, "You sure look nice today."

5. *Loss of identity*: To a widow or widower life can seem meaningless and very lonely. When they observe couples pairing off at social events they get the feeling they no longer fit in. They are like a square peg in a round hole. When a person who was accustomed to sharing life with a spouse suddenly faces the future alone, it's easy to experience days, even years, of feelings of unacceptance. Just a note or telephone call could make their day brighter.[13]

To willingly become actively involved in an older person's life is a major commitment of time and energy. It can be emotionally draining if you are not prepared to interact with them. McKinney says, "Most of all, ask the Holy Spirit to make you a blessing, and He will instruct you with what to say and to whom it should be said."[14]

ONE CHURCH'S EXAMPLE: VALUE STATEMENTS

Monte Vista Chapel is a nondenominational church located in Turlock, California. Its origins come out of the Covenant church. The beginnings of Monte Vista Chapel came as a result of a departure from the Turlock Beulah Covenant church (now the Turlock Covenant church) in 1966. In the intervening years there has been a good deal of growth. However, those who were young at the beginning are in the elderly category now. It has been necessary to reevaluate the purpose and mission in light of many changes. The church has grown from 300 to over 1200 in those years. The population of the town has increased fivefold. The ethnic population has shifted from primarily those of Scandinavian descent to significant numbers of Assyrians, Hispanics, Portuguese, and Sikhs. As a result, the church leadership has rewritten its value statements to include the following pronouncements.

- People are important and their most basic need is fellowship with God.
- Our presentation of the message must be culturally relevant.
- The role of the church is to support and reinforce the family as God's basic unit in society. The family is responsible for the spiritual, emotional, and physical development of its members.[15]

At first glance the value statement that people are important may appear obvious if not a bit ludicrous. However, with attitudes toward the elderly often being poor or negative (see Chapter 4), it was determined that the church needed to establish a straightforward statement proclaiming the worth of every individual. Senior pastor, Dr. Roy Price, said in one of his sermons on the family that "the family is responsible for the development of its members. The church is to support the family, not be a substitute. As the primary source of biblical teaching the church also informs the home of biblical standards, so there is interaction between the two."[16]

NOTES

1. Robert Alexander, "Religion and the Aging Person," in *Help! I'm Parenting My Parents*, ed. Jamia Jasper Jacobsen (Indianapolis: Benchmark Press, 1988), 94.
2. Ibid.
3. Ibid.
4. David L. Rambo, *Briefing* [Monthly newsletter], May 1994.
5. Alexander, 95.
6. Ibid., 96.
7. Ibid.
8. Ibid., 97.
9. Ibid.
10. "Death and Dying: The Role of the Church Secretary as Caregiver," *Church Secretary's Communique* [Christian Ministry Resources, Matthews, N.C.], Oct. 1994, 1.
11."Life Begins at 80," *Escalon Heritage House Herald*, Escalon, Calif., April 1997, 4.

12. Eleanor McKinney, "The Top Five Concerns of the Aging," *Just Between Us*, Fall 1996, 20.

13. Ibid.

14. Ibid.

15. "Basic Values Statement," Monte Vista Chapel, Turlock, Calif., 1994.

16. Roy C. Price, *We Value the Family, Encouragement and Leadership*, series on The Relationship of the Family to the Church, Monte Vista Chapel, Turlock, Calif., 20 Nov. 1994.

VII

Education and the Sandwich Generation:
A Blueprint

Because the sandwich generation is a new phenomena, and an ongoing dilemma, education is essential for those in the midst of the dilemma, or who are seeing the possibilities of it in the future.

A course of study designed to last twelve weeks in a normal hourly Sunday school setting is presented for consideration. When this idea was suggested to my dialogue group, all of them indicated they would be interested in attending, or even taking part. Others said they knew people who would want to take the course, these people being those who also find themselves in the sandwich generation. One man in the group, who hails from Guatemala, cleverly coined a new phrase to describe the sandwich generation. He proposed we call it the "taco generation." We all enjoyed a laugh at that, and even now some of us will use the term "taco" generation, always with a smile.

The primary text for the course would be Jamia Jasper Jacobsen's book, *Help! I'm Parenting My Parents*. This course would draw from the bibliography in this professional project, bring in outside speakers who are experts in their field, and utilize an informal small group approach to encourage interaction with the material. Discussion starters, listed under each week's topic, would facilitate personal involvement. The curriculum would cover the following areas in order to offer a brief but complete understanding of the sandwich generation.

A TWELVE-WEEK COURSE

Week 1
A History of Parent Care
- Overview of the Sandwich Generation Phenomena
- Emphasis on ethnic values and diversity
- Discussion Starters: Why the need for such a class?
- What can I hope to gain from this class? Why do I feel so helpless in trying to provide for my parents?

Week 2
The Bible and Parent Care
- Honor Thy Father and Thy Mother: inductive study
- Consider biblical examples of parent care
- Discussion Starters: What is our church doing about parent care? Where does the bible place the responsibility for parent care? What circumstances are unique to my situation?

Week 3
Interfacing with the Chronologically Gifted
- Presentation by the Director of Senior Adult Ministries (including Q & A)
- Small group discussion with the elderly
- Discussion Starters: How would you want to be cared for? Would you expect to be cared for by your adult children? To what degree? Have you discussed this with your family?

Week 4
Requirements for Providing Parent Care
- Understanding your own background and temperament
- Taking a serious look at commitment
- Discussion Starters: Where am I in being able to care for my parent(s)? What resources are available (family, finances, community, insurance)? How do I personally feel about taking care of my parent(s)?

Week 5
Knowing What is Available
- Community agency representatives to share
- Know the law
- Discussion Starters: What's out there to help me in parent care? Is placing my parent(s) in a retirement/nursing home an option? Has my parent(s) stated their wishes on this matter?

Week 6
The Church and Parent Care
- Work with what presently exists
- Develop a task force to explore possible ministries
- Discussion Starters: How should I be involved? Are there any other churches in the area that are addressing this issue? Do I need to consider having my parent(s) move here to provide better care and supervision? Could the church start a hospice program, not just for the church, but for the community?

Week 7
Confronting the Hard Decisions (Part 1)
- Medical Professional presentation (Alzheimer's, euthanasia, right to die, when to "pull the plug")
- Role play various scenarios
- Discussion Starters: How will I ever make such horrendous decisions? Have I discussed these issues with my parent(s)? Are there any theological complications in the decision making, i.e., do I take all measures available to keep my loved one alive? Do I allow for blood transfusions? Will my wishes and beliefs override those of my loved one if they are no longer able to communicate those wishes?

Week 8
Confronting the Hard Decisions (Part 2)
- Financial Planner to address the need to work with present finances and to plan for future eventualities, entitlements, etc.

- Small group discussion
- Discussion Starters: Can I possibly save enough to cover future expenses? Has an executor been named in writing? Are all family members aware of the wishes of the parent(s)? Would it not be wiser and more fiscally responsible to take care of funeral arrangements now while everyone is emotionally calm? Is such a discussion with family members even realistic? Has a durable power of attorney been made out?

Week 9
Confronting the Hard Decisions (Part 3)
- Wills, living wills, trusts and other matters of personal concern and disbursement
- Small group discussion
- Discussion Starters: What sort of will do I need? To whom do I leave an inheritance? Won't such decisions only cause dissension in the family?

Week 10
Field trip to a Local Nursing Home
(This will require more than the one hour, finishing up with lunch together either at the nursing home, or at a local restaurant where discussion of what folks experienced on the field trip could be entertained)
Discussion Starters: What impressions did you come away with that were positive? Negative? Reflecting back upon your comments early in the course about placing a loved one in such a place, do you still feel the same way? Why? Why not? What arrangements would you want to make now?

Week 11
Where to go from here
This final class will be an opportunity to review and rehash all that was covered in the course using an open forum to encourage dialogue. An evaluation form of the course will be handed out for purposes of improving the course. Discussion would also center on

the text for the course, Help! I'm Parenting My Parents, edited by Jamia Jasper Jacobsen.

Week 12

Family Meeting (Optional)

This class would be an opportunity for families to meet together to discuss the issues presented throughout the course. Multiple generations within the family would be encouraged to participate. A list of discussion questions would be provided to guide the meeting, along with forms to fill out in the process of organizing and filing all the necessary documents for wills, estates, stocks, bonds, personal accounts, distribution of heirlooms, and generally anything of importance or value to the individual.

The class would most likely be taught once a year in the church. However, it could have a broader outreach to the community if advertised properly through radio and newspaper. This is a much needed ministry within our communities.

LIFESTORIES: ALL IN THE FAMILY

Another source of education for the sandwich generation is the board game, LifeStories. "'It's a game about affirmation, about stories that generations can share,' said Vivian Elaine Johnson, one of the creators of LifeStories."[1] Johnson made good use of her background in behavioral science in creating the game. She says the game is also being used in some unusual places, such as drug rehabilitation programs, family reunions, and in corporate team-building.

Players move around a board, pick up various cards and answer questions about memories and special moments in their lives. The emphasis is on sharing—preferably through richly moral tales. . . . LifeStories grew from a conviction by Johnson and her partners that family histories were disappearing. One of her favorite quotes is a remark by "Roots" author Alex Haley: "When an old person dies, it's like a small library burning." Memories are lost because they are not shared. "Nobody talks anymore in this television era," Johnson said. "People need help."[2]

JUST IN CASE

In a booklet entitled, "To My Loved Ones . . . JUST IN CASE," my friend and fellow minister, Dr. Gordon F. Rasmussen, compiled an excellent resource for everyone to leave for their families. It is full of information to be filled out by each individual in the eventuality of their death. The booklet is broken down into nine sections.

1. Personal Notes
2. Important Records
   Marriage Records
   Birth and Citizenship Papers
   Education
   Military Service
   Veterans Organization
   Estate Plan
3. Finances
   Bank Accounts
   Safe Deposit Box
   Outstanding Loans and Debts
   Accounts Receivable
   Credit Cards
   Tax Information
   Investments
   Retirement Plans
4. Insurance
   Life Insurance
   Other Insurance Policies
5. Property & Valuables
   Real Estate Owned
   Vehicles
   Personal Property & Valuables
   Private Information
6. Funeral Arrangements
   Funeral Cost Information

Additional Considerations
7. Contact in Emergencies
8. Survivor's Guide
    What to Expect
    What to do First
    Things to be Done by the Family
9. Additional Space[3]

This booklet is designed to fit into a file or a safe deposit box along with other personal documents. A person who fills this out has saved their family the enormous task of attempting to track down all the pertinent information needed at the time of the loved one's death. The individual's wishes are stated clearly as to what they want done with their possessions, the kind of service they want for their funeral, among other final matters in closing the estate of a family member. (See *Appendices*, page 121, for information on obtaining copies of this booklet.)

DOES CARING EVER STOP?

This is the question that plays on the mind of the caregiver, particularly the family member who is burdened with the ongoing care of an elderly parent(s). There is good news. A number of factors allow for significant positive change in the way families care for their elderly. But care will always be required, and it will be for the life of the individual. Dychtwald, in his book *Age Wave*, presents the Matrix Family as adult-centered. Borrowing from modern organizational theory, he makes use of the matrix configuration in describing the matrix family differently from the norm of the past.

- *Adult-centered.* With declining fertility, extending longevity, and the rise in median age we are experiencing, the majority of family relations are no longer between young children and adults, but between adults and adults.

- *Transgenerational.* Relationships that combine, cross, and even skip generations become increasingly possible in our long-lived era.
- *Bound together by friendship and choice as well as by blood and obligation.* With increasing lifestyle independence and mobility, friendship and shared concerns become as much the basis for family-type relationships as bloodline.[4]

Five social and lifestyle factors are given in explaining the emergence of the sandwich generation.

- *Longer lives*—those over 85 are the ones most in need of care, and are also the fastest-growing segment of the population.
- *Chronic disease*—today older people suffer longer with diseases because they are not always life threatening.
- *Lower ratio of children to parents*—the number of adults available as caretakers is shrinking due to lower numbers of children per family.
- *The great increase in widowhood*—the gap has opened up between the life expectancies of men and women.
- *Increased entry of women of caregiving age into the labor force*—more women are pursuing careers, making it more difficult to provide daily care for aging parents.[5]

The reality of long-term care of elderly parents is not without its problems. One recent study showed that parent-caring is becoming a moodier source of stress in family life.[6] As a society we can no longer practice care for the elderly as in days gone by. It will require a team effort involving more than one generation willing to pitch in financially, physically, emotionally and spiritually.

A poem written by Rae Turnbull speaks eloquently of the respect and admiration she has for her mother's courage in the face of life's more challenging times.

Over the years,
my mother and I
have known each other
in our best

and worst times.
And I've marveled often
at her strong ability
to meet life's challenges
with a courage
few can claim.

Fight and heart
have always been
her very stock in trade.
It's not her way
to just accept
the cards she's dealt
without a valiant effort
to change them
in her favor.

But this deck
she deals with now
leaves little room
for rearranging.
Yet she bravely
plays this hand
with a calm
and steady grace.

And I am once again
amazed
by this woman
God has given me
the honor to call Mother.[7]

So, does caring ever stop? In a word, no. The sandwich generation is here to stay. The church needs to be a companion who comes alongside the individual or family needing assistance in parent-care. Such an opportunity to minister to the community should be aggressively pursued. Surely Jesus' words in Matthew 25:40, "Whatever you did for one of the least of these brothers of mine, you did for me," would be appropriately applied to the church taking steps in helping the sandwich generation.

NOTES

1. Jane Ellen Haas, "Generations Learn from Each Other in Board Game," *Turlock* [Calif.] *Journal*, 18 Jan. 1995, A5.

2. Ibid.

3. Gordon F. Rasmussen, *To My Loved Ones . . . JUST IN CASE*, Turlock, Calif., 1997.

4. Dychtwald, 235-36.

5. Ibid., 238-39.

6. Ibid., 243.

7. Rae Turnbull, a poem, *Modesto* [Calif.] *Bee*, 12 May 1997, D1.

VIII
Conclusion and Analysis

The findings in current research on the elderly now contradict a number of beliefs long held in American society, the most dominant one being that the sandwich generation should be taking care of the elderly. This, in spite of the fact that people are living significantly longer, and the costs involved in caring for the aged are already astronomically high. Another belief that has been disproved is that the elderly want to retire and "play," or just sit around and do nothing. Though the evidence is in, it will take a long time to begin to change people's minds about the elderly, if ever.

A story I found very encouraging was that of a 93-year-old lady and her imaginative entrepreneurial spirit. Florence Foster needed the use of a walking cane if she was to go hiking with her daughter in Arizona, but that ugly, gray metal thing the hospital gave her? Forget it. "You use a cane like that, people will start treating you like you're old."

Foster had a better idea. She went to an auto parts factory down the road in Jackson, Michigan - just strolled in off the street - and told them what she needed. A clear plastic tube, about 1 1/4 inches in diameter. A rubber tip at one end. A handle.

Can do, the company said. Then she took her cane to a crafts store, yanked off the rubber tip and filled the tube with a string of little silk roses. Presto: A fine and fashionable accessory she could take even to a wedding, "though of course, you might steal the show from the bride."

You want to call Florence Foster vain, go right ahead. But last year, she invented a better cane.

Now - at 93 - she's selling it.[1]

Florence Foster now has a business earning a nice profit from the manufacture of customized walking canes. She suggests that men pull out the silk flowers and put in golf tees, or maybe fishing lures. Kids who need a cane might want to put in plastic figurines or brightly colored rubber snakes. She still hates for anyone to think she's feeble or infirm. Truth is, she doesn't use her cane around the house. It's just for the uneven spots outdoors. She even drives her friends to the store or out to social events.[2]

But families will continue to be the primary caregivers to the elderly, except that the government will most likely assume the economic burden associated with an aging population. Case in point, the current administrations strong efforts to pass through Congress a national health care bill. Allowing senior citizens to remain employed instead of forcing upon them mandatory retirement, will, undoubtedly, help ease the economic burden, and continue to give the elderly a sense of purpose and importance within society as well as the family. Added to that is the possibility of the easing of the social security restrictions proposed by the current Congress as mentioned in Chapter 3.

The need for family members to sit down and discuss the wishes of aging parents, and the role to be played by the sandwich generation, cannot be stressed strongly enough. Contingency plans should be written out with the full cognizance of all family members. Obviously not everything can be anticipated, but a working plan, one that's in place, could prevent the major difficulties that increasingly arise today in the care of the elderly. The sandwich generation and the future multiple sandwiching of generations will only serve to highlight the importance of family communication. The matrix model, where the family works together as a team, is the best course of action in resolving the issues engulfing an overburdened family structure.

The elderly are not just fearful of their own demise, but of experiencing a degeneration in the quality of life they had once known and experienced. As the reality of their own aging process takes hold, the elderly person often goes through the steps of grief seen most often in progressive stages. The stages may become jumbled at times, but the journey from denial to the inevitability of being resigned to their declining humanity does not have to be fraught with fear if they are surrounded by friends and family who love them and are there to be of support. If this support is not present, inordinate fears may develop, leading to a form of pathological grief.[3]

In today's cultural climate, respect is not automatically given to the elderly. Instead, it has to be earned, which is difficult for many older Americans due to cultural upbringing and societal norms established and reinforced by previous generations. However, we can teach children to honor and respect the elderly at home, in our schools, and in the church. It must be a concentrated effort by everyone. It will not happen overnight. It will not happen in a decade. But we must do what we can now so that change in thought and action will come later. If we fail to act now, we will surely fail to assist the elderly in their final years. Then, what about us? How will we be viewed by those coming behind us? And how will our children be viewed when they reach old age? And their children? The time to act is now.

NOTES

1. Neal Rubin, "93-Year -Old's Vanity Led to a Better Cane," *Modesto* [Calif.] *Bee*, 7 Jul. 1997, D-3.

2. Ibid.

3. David K. Switzer, "Grief and Loss," in *Dictionary of Pastoral Care and Counseling*, ed. Rodney J. Hunter (Nashville: Abingdon Press, 1990), 472.

IX
Summary

My mother has shared with me her involvement with organizations specifically geared to the elderly. Besides her participation in the Triple L Club at her former church, she belongs to the Older Americans Organization—Senior Partners. This is a volunteer service credit program that allows people to assist elderly persons in need, and by so doing they earn points for themselves. They may then donate their credit to someone else, donate the credit back to Senior Partners to be distributed as needed, or donate the credit to a group pool where group members may use the credit as needed. There are four different types of service provided.

- *Personal Support* includes sewing and mending, reading, telephone reassurance, assistance with grooming, etc.
- *Household Support* includes light housework or yard work, non-strenuous home repair, simple meal preparation, etc.
- *Community Support* includes transportation, escorting to the doctor, shopping, recreation, etc.
- *Program Support* includes assisting with office work, volunteer recruitment, follow-up tasks, telephone work, etc.[1]

Before he passed away, my father managed to take advantage of his vast experience in the corporate world by offering services to an organization known as SCORE (Service Corps of Retired Executives), the volunteer arm of the SBA (Small Business Association). These retired persons provide counsel, support and encouragement to small business owners, or those interested in starting their own business. Seminars, tax assistance, and on-the-spot analysis are just some of the many services that SCORE provides. My father felt that he made a positive contribution to the community he and my mother lived in by making a difference in the economic industry of that community. He was able to stay active in business and pass on to others what he had learned in a lifetime in marketing. He performed in this capacity until his death at age eighty. A motto for SCORE sums up their contribution: "A rich lode of experience dedicated to improving small business."[2]

As for my grandmother, Bambi, she died at age 94. In fact, her funeral was the first I performed as an ordained minister. She lived in my parents home until she was 93. The last couple of years she deteriorated rapidly in mind, eventually failing to remember any of her immediate family members. Alzheimer's had come to stay. She did not want to go into a nursing home, but as a family we felt it was the best course of action to take. My parents were well past 65 at the time, and were experiencing physical difficulties which hampered their ability to care for my grandmother the way they felt they should. My wife and I took her in with us for a number of weeks, but we had two small children at the time, a three-year-old, and a six-month-old. We constantly worried about Bambi wandering off alone (which she was prone to do), or falling and being seriously hurt. She had become very unsteady on her feet. My wife and I finally met with my parents and made arrangements for Bambi to be placed in a local nursing home. It was, undoubtedly, the most difficult and heart-wrenching decision of my life. I was devastated by this course of action, but I knew it must be done. Bambi died less than a year later.

My mother, now 82, is doing wonderfully, and continues to provide several days a month as a volunteer at the local hospital in the surgical ward, and as a volunteer teacher with the Adult Literacy Program. She travels about visiting children and grandchildren with seemingly nary a care, and recently returned from a month long trip to France to visit an old friend. Will she one day need assistance from her offspring? Probably. But who knows? Regardless of what may come, I'm ready!

NOTES

1. *Senior Partners: A Volunteer Service Credit Program*, flier published by Older Americans Organization, 1028 N. Fulton St., Fresno, Calif., 93728, n.d.

2. From *The Savant*, a publication of SCORE, sponsored by U.S. Small Business Administration, Washington, D.C., Jan. 1991.